HAUNTED HOTELS OF MICHIGAN

HAUNTED HOTELS OF MICHIGAN

ROXANNE RHOADS

Haunted
America

Published by Haunted America
A Division of The History Press
Charleston, SC
www.historypress.com

First published 2024

Manufactured in the United States

ISBN 9781467157858

Library of Congress Control Number: 2024936726

To my children, Tim, Ari, and Robby Napolitano—
The three of you are my driving force.
I love you more than you could possibly know.

CONTENTS

Exploring Energy and Hauntings in Liminal Spaces

D eath is universal, yet not all places seem to echo with its lingering presence. Why do some locations become filled with the whispers of restless souls, while others seem to remain untouched by the spectral world? Perhaps the answer lies not just in the dead but in the living—in the energy we leave behind, the echoes of history embedded in the walls, and the way our own senses filter the unseen world—so one explanation might lie within a complex combination of energy, environment, and human perception.

Imagine a spectrum of energy, encompassing all living things. When life flickers out, this energy doesn't vanish; it transforms. For most, it flows onward, moving on to the next realm. But for some, it gets caught, tangled in threads of unfinished business, trauma, or even fear of the unknown. These trapped energies, echoes of lives abruptly cut short, might imprint themselves on certain locations, leaving behind ghostly fingerprints. Think of a traumatic event, potent with emotion, replaying on a loop in your mind. Now imagine that energy imprinted on a physical space, a hotel room perhaps, where the tragedy unfolded.

We are beings of energy, and after death, that essence doesn't simply vanish. Some believe certain spirits leave a mark, an imprint of their emotional turmoil etched into the fabric of a location. Like a record stuck on repeat, their anguish plays out in chilling echoes, haunting the halls of memory. This residual energy could manifest in ways perceptible to those sensitive enough—flickering lights, whispers in the night, unexplained chills.

Each spirit may vibrate on a different frequency, a conscious hum that allows interaction with the living. This explains why certain individuals, often those with heightened sensitivity, can perceive what others cannot. It's like tuning a radio, able to pick up frequencies beyond the usual range. Some are tuned to the static hum of the everyday, while others, with their sensitivity amplified by neurodiversity or environmental factors, can pick up faint, otherworldly signals.

People who are neurodiverse, like those on the autism spectrum or those with ADHD, often display a remarkable ability to perceive the paranormal. Studies suggest their enhanced awareness of their surroundings bleeds into the realm of the unseen, making them more susceptible to ghostly encounters.

Liminal spaces become canvases where our fears and anxieties mingle with the whispers of the past. It's a potent cocktail that can ignite the imagination and leave even the most skeptical feeling a chill down their spine. This explains why transitional zones like hotels are frequent haunts. Hotels exist on the threshold between the familiar and the unknown. They are temporary havens, holding echoes of countless lives. They blur boundaries, thinning the veil between worlds and inviting the unseen to linger. This in-betweenness, echoing the Jungian concept of the collective unconscious, can trigger primal anxieties, making us feel unsettled.

Perhaps, then, hauntings are not solely about vengeful spirits or restless souls. Maybe they are a confluence of factors—trapped energy, sensitive individuals, and liminal spaces that amplify our perception of the unseen. This doesn't diminish the chills that crawl down our spines, but it adds a layer of intrigue, suggesting that hauntings are not just supernatural anomalies but windows into the complex interplay between mind, environment, and the lingering energy of life.

This fascination with the unseen has drawn me to the world of haunted hotels. Their odd energy, a blend of history, human emotion, and liminal space, invites us to explore the echoes of history and restless spirits trapped within their walls.

ACKNOWLEDGEMENTS

First of all, I want to thank my husband, Robert, for trekking all over the state with me to visit the hotels featured in this book. I really enjoyed our adventures together.

Thank you to my Obsidian sisters, Samantha and Laura, for always being there for me, listening to my troubles, and boosting my morale when things got rough. You guys are the best!

I also want to thank everyone who took the time to answer my questions and provide details for the book—hotel owners, managers, staff, paranormal investigators, and so on. Thank you so much for your help creating *Haunted Hotels of Michigan*. I couldn't have done it without you.

And last but not least, a huge thank-you to John Rodrigue for publishing my third book with The History Press.

Introduction
Liminal Spaces

*the ghosts that haunt us
betwixt and between,
lingering in two worlds
here but unseen*

Have you ever stood in a place where time stood still, where the familiar melted into the unknown and the air crackled with anticipation? This is the essence of a liminal space.

These in-between realms, neither here nor there, exist in the whispers of ancient hallways, the dust-laden attics, and the echoing stairwells of Michigan's haunted hotels. Here, within the aged walls, the past clings to the present, and the living brush shoulders with the spectral echoes of yesterday.

Imagine stepping into a lobby once abuzz with laughter and chatter, now draped in an eerie silence. The grandfather clock ticks a mournful rhythm. In the distance, a faint melody drifts from a ballroom, a ghostly waltz beckoning from a forgotten era.

As you wander down echoing corridors, shadows dance in the flickering light, revealing glimpses of figures long departed. A child's laughter drifts through the halls, a phantom memory of joy that lingers even in the darkness.

Open a creaky old door and enter a room where time seems to have warped. Furniture from the past mingles with modern technology, while faded photographs gaze down from the walls, their subjects frozen in time. The air hangs heavy with secrets lost to history.

But these are not just empty spaces; they are portals to the beyond. Here, the veil between worlds thins, allowing the spectral residents to linger, their unfinished business tethered to the earthly realm.

Let us delve into the heart of Michigan's liminal spaces, where history whispers, spirits roam, and the boundary between life and death blurs, hinting at the captivating mysteries hidden within the walls of these old buildings.

Who knows what secrets we may uncover? Perhaps we'll hear the mournful lament of a heartbroken lover, witness the playful antics of a mischievous child, or feel the chilling touch of a presence unseen.

Join me on this journey as we visit the haunted hotels of Michigan.

PART I
WHERE WILDERNESS MEETS WATER

MICHIGAN'S UPPER PENINSULA

The Upper Peninsula of Michigan features dense forests nestled between three of the Great Lakes. It is a wild frontier connected to the mainland by the slender thread of the Mackinac Bridge. From the days of fur trappers and traders to modern-day adventurers, the Upper Peninsula of Michigan has beckoned with its wild allure.

Imagine a land carved by ancient glaciers, cloaked in emerald forests, and surrounded by Great Lakes—over 1,700 miles of continuous shoreline. That's the Upper Peninsula of Michigan, a rugged wonderland barely touched by time. It spans approximately 370 miles from end to end, coming in at around 16,500 square miles. It is approximately one-third of the total land mass of the state of Michigan, but it holds only 3 percent of the population.

The UP, as Michiganders affectionately call it, is a world apart from Michigan's bustling Lower Peninsula. It's a realm of soaring cliffs overlooking Lake Superior, hidden waterfalls tucked away in pristine woods, and charming towns where time seems to stand still, or at least slow down to a crawl, while the rest of the world has moved on with lightning-fast speed. Forget neon lights and crowded streets. The UP is a symphony of starlit nights, crackling campfires, and the rhythmic crash of waves against rocky shores.

The Upper Peninsula's haunting beauty is enhanced by its layers of history and the grip of its long winters. Desolate

The Mackinac Bridge.

stretches of road, where towns feel miles apart and gas stations become elusive mirages, add a chilling atmosphere to the already captivating landscape. Crumbling resorts and abandoned attractions stand as skeletal sentinels, whispering tales of past summers and faded laughter. They paint a picture of a bygone era, when tourism thrived and then mysteriously retreated, leaving these structures to be reclaimed by the wilds of the land.

But then you reach the major cities of the UP, their buildings layered with history. They've witnessed generations and industries come and go. Their walls absorbed laughter and tears, whispers of triumph and tragedy. Now they seem eager to spill their secrets. You might catch a glimpse of a ghostly bellhop from a long-defunct resort or hear the echoes of laughter from a forgotten summer night. Ghosts wander the land freely. Several of the lighthouses in the UP have a resident spirit or two, including Marquette Harbor Lighthouse, Seul Choix, Whitefish Point, and Big Bay. Northern Michigan University has numerous spirits that haunt the halls.

Many of the most haunted locations have ties to the 1952 murder that happened in Big Bay and the 1959 movie that dramatized it, *Anatomy of a Murder*. The Lumberjack Tavern in Big Bay, where the murder occurred, showcases memorabilia and newspaper clippings from both the murder and the iconic film. The film's logo is painted on the floor, marking the place where the body hit the ground after being shot. Visitors can also see real bullet holes in the wall and ask to see the actual murder weapon.

The UP is a storyteller. If you listen closely, it will regale you with tales both haunting and beautiful.

CHAPTER 1
A HAUNTING TALE OF LOST LOVE

THE NAHMA INN, RAPID RIVER

13747 MAIN STREET, NAHMA, MI 49864

Logging was once a major industry in Michigan's Upper Peninsula. The industry gained steam due to the demands of fur traders in the early 1800s. By the mid-1800s, logging had become the dominant industry in upper Michigan as immigrants moved in and the need for lumber increased. Thanks to rivers and streams that could move lumber quickly, logging towns popped up all over the Upper Peninsula. Nahma was one of those towns.

The Bay de Noquet Lumber Company opened in 1881 with over 1,200 employees, over 800 of whom lived in Nahma. The Nahma Inn was built in 1909 for Bay de Noquet employees. Charlie Good, the president of the Bay de Noquet lumber company, was a frequent guest. Whispered rumors said he and a member of the kitchen staff, Nell Fleming, had a steamy love affair. That relationship was destined for disaster. One day, Charlie left and never came back. Poor Nell was heartbroken; she had fallen madly in love with Charlie. Devastated by his departure, she would often stare out her second-floor window hoping that one day she would see him returning to her.

Years later, guests of the Nahma still see Nell's ghostly form watching for Charlie from that window. Guests who stay in Nell's old room often discover their things have been moved around and the lights turn off and on by themselves. Paranormal investigators have caught the sound of a woman's laughter in their EVP recordings. When Nell is not in her room, she can be found in the hotel kitchen cleaning and reorganizing, creating havoc for the current staff, who can't find anything when they come to work in the mornings.

Nell is just one of the spirits roaming the Nahma Inn. Some think Charlie Good is there, too. But if that's the case, why is Nell still searching for him? You would think they'd connect and continue their affair in the afterlife. Perhaps his spirit still thinks their love is forbidden and even though he returned to be close to her, he avoids reuniting with her in the afterlife.

Footsteps are often heard coming from the empty second floor, along with the eerie echo of someone singing lullabies. A ghostly girl around ten years old has been seen on multiple occasions. Coins fall like cursed raindrops from the heavens, knives and spoons defy gravity, and glasses shatter under the grip of invisible fingers.

One guest was kept up all night by a ghostly party. The lounge echoed with raucous laughter, yet when confronted, the noisemakers vanished like smoke in the night, leaving only the sense of unseen eyes lingering in the shadows, watching him as he returned to his room tired and confused.

The Nahma Inn is a place where love and longing intertwine, where the past refuses to release its grip on the present and ghostly figures continue to linger among the living.

CHAPTER 2

LILACS AND LOST LOVE

UNVEILING THE SPIRITS OF THE LANDMARK INN, MARQUETTE

230 NORTH FRONT STREET, MARQUETTE, MI 49855

Iron mining was another major industry in upper Michigan. Remnants of iron mining can still be found throughout the Upper Peninsula, especially in Marquette, the UP's oldest town. The Northland Hotel was built for workers of the iron industry.

By the time the Northland opened in January 1930, Marquette was already a bustling town on Lake Superior's shore. Celebrities, politicians, and foreign dignitaries passing through town all stayed there. Among these were Amelia Earhart, Abbott and Costello, Duke Ellington, Louis Armstrong, and members of the Rolling Stones. During the 1959 filming of *Anatomy of a Murder*, the cast and crew stayed at the Northland, including Jimmy Stewart.

By the late 1970s, the hotel had fallen on hard times. It closed its doors in 1982. It remained empty until 1995, when it was purchased and rehabilitated. It reopened as the Landmark Inn, once again becoming the destination for VIP guests, including the Rolling Stones, who returned to the hotel in 2002.

The basis for some of the ghost stories started before the hotel was even finished in the early twentieth century. It took thirteen years to complete, and for many years, it sat partially completed, which attracted certain types of businessmen and ladies of the night. They would use the unfinished rooms to conduct "business deals." Rumors say one customer was not happy with a certain lady, and he murdered her in a fit of rage and buried her in the basement. Construction workers complained of hearing a woman crying,

Before it was the Landmark, it was the Northland.

screaming, or whispering to them. Perhaps her spirit was urging them to find her body so she could be laid to rest properly.

Another haunting was created from love, not murder. A local librarian fell in love with a sailor. Whenever he came to town, they would meet at the Landmark. They made plans to marry and settle in town after the sailor's last trip. Unfortunately, he never came home from that final trip. His ship was one of many that met its end in the treacherous stormy waters of Lake Superior and ended up at the bottom of the frigid lake. The poor librarian could never recover from the loss and hanged herself in her sixth-floor room.

That room is now known as the Lilac Room. The nameless librarian supposedly loved lilacs, and her spirit is often seen wearing a dress with lilac print. The sounds of a woman crying can be heard in the room. Guests report their things often are moved around. The first guest who stayed after the renovations were complete found screws between his sheets. After staff removed the screws, he found more there later in the day.

Ghostly calls to the front desk come from the empty Lilac Room quite often. Staff members report an eerie silence emanating from the phone when they pick it up.

Men who stay in the room have experienced strange things like waking up to the bright sun blinding them even though they know they went to sleep with the blinds closed. Many staff members refuse to go to the sixth floor at night.

CHAPTER 3

BOOTLEGGERS, BOOZE, AND RESTLESS SPIRITS

THE HOUSE OF LUDINGTON, ESCANABA

223 LUDINGTON STREET, ESCANABA, MI 49829

Near the shores of Little Bay de Noc in Escanaba stands the Great White Castle, the Lady of the Lakefront—a hotel that exemplified the Queen Anne resort architecture that was very popular in the 1880s and 1890s.

The House of Ludington opened in 1865 as the Gaynor House Hotel, built by lumber baron E. Gaynor. The house was originally located in the middle of Ludington Street. It was moved to its current location in 1868.

The hotel was renamed the Ludington House in 1871 after lumberman Nelson Ludington. In 1883, John Christie purchased the hotel, renaming it the New Ludington Hotel. Christie added a west wing in 1903. By 1910, the hotel had over one hundred rooms.

In 1939, Pat Hayes purchased the hotel. Legends say that Hayes was connected to the Chicago mob. He worked as host, chef, and manager of the property. It was said Hayes helped put Escanaba on the map. "The house that Pat built" is what the *Detroit Magazine* called the Ludington in a feature story written by Robert Traver. (Robert Traver was the pseudonym of former Michigan Supreme Court justice John D. Voelker, author of *Anatomy of a Murder*.)

Hayes was well known for his Irish temper and his refusal to serve anyone a well-done steak. If a well-done steak was ordered, that person would get fish, chicken, or a boot right out of the place.

House of Ludington.

Hayes installed Michigan's first glass elevator in 1959 after fighting with the city over it for quite some time. He even threatened to guard the installation himself with a shotgun if anyone tried to interfere.

Rumor has it Hayes was a friend of Al Capone's and used the hotel's three basements and tunnels for all sorts of illegal activities, including the storage of the mob's bootleg booze. That booze and possibly other "things" might still be down there in the tunnels somewhere.

In 1969, Hayes died in the hotel from prostate cancer. Some say he never left. The glass elevator remains and tends to go up and down on its own, with no one inside—at least not anyone who can be seen. Is Pat still traveling the floors in his glass elevator?

There are many reports of a tobacco-reeking crabby spirit with horrible body odor that creeps around the hotel. In addition, phantom footsteps creak on the stairs every day at exactly 5:15 a.m., rocking chairs rock on their own, and furniture often rearranges itself. But the oddest thing is the angel that finds its way to the top of the Christmas tree every year with no help from human hands.

CHAPTER 4

ANATOMY OF A HAUNTING

GHOST STORIES AND MURDER AT BIG BAY POINT LIGHTHOUSE, BIG BAY

4674 COUNTY ROAD KCB, BIG BAY, MI 49808

Big Bay Point is one of the only Michigan lighthouses that had been transformed into a bed-and-breakfast. Imagine watching the incredible sunrise and sunset views overlooking Lake Superior from this beautifully restored lighthouse. During your stay, you might even encounter the ghosts that are said to haunt this historic brick structure.

Big Bay Point Lighthouse sits at the end of a narrow point in Michigan's Upper Peninsula around twenty-five miles northwest of Marquette. The lighthouse was completed in October 1896. The brick building was a duplex to house the light keeper, the assistant to the keeper, and their families. The lighthouse tower stands 105 feet over the rocky shores of Lake Superior.

Harry William Prior (sometimes spelled Pryor) was the first light keeper. His journal and notes indicate he took his job very seriously and expected others to do the same. He was very disciplined and set in his ways; his assistants were not. His journals noted that he was not pleased with their work. Time after time, assistants kept disappointing him.

He finally became so fed up that he put assistant George Beamer on a steamer and sent him away in November 1898. He then appointed his nineteen-year-old son George Edward (sometimes listed as Edward George) to the assistant light keeper position. They worked together without incident for around fifteen months until April 1901, when George fell and hurt his

Big Bay Point Lighthouse.

leg. He cut it on the stone steps, all the way to the bone. The injury was so bad that he was taken to St. Mary's Hospital in Marquette.

On April 18, Prior noted in his log that "he [George] will have to remain in hospital for treatment." Young Prior battled gangrene but could not recover. It took his life. On June 13, Prior wrote in his log, "1:30 p.m. Keeper summoned to Marquette to bury his son who died this morning."

Prior slipped into a deep depression after his son's death. He was despondent, and his journal entries dwindled. Rumor has it he disappeared into the woods on June 28, 1901, with a shotgun and some strychnine. Everyone feared the worst. He seemed to have just vanished. He never came back to the lighthouse, and no one could find him. His wife, Mary, and their four younger children left on a boat heading to Marquette in the fall of 1901.

Frederick Babcock had no idea what was in store when he packed up to go hunting in the woods one day in November 1902. Trekking through the woods with his gear, Babcock stumbled upon a horrific sight: a weather- and animal-ravaged skeleton hanging from a tree. Tattered shreds of fabric that were once a lighthouse keeper's uniform clung to the bones, and a few tufts of red hair still clung to the skull. It had been seventeen months since Prior disappeared.

Babcock ran to the lighthouse to report what he had found. The old logbook noted his report: "Mr. Fred Babcock came to the station 12:30 pm. While hunting in the woods one and a half-miles south of the station this noon he found a skeleton of a man hanging to a tree. We went to the place with him and found that the clothing and everything tally with the former keeper of this station who has been missing for seventeen months."

In November 1902, the *Mining Journal* reported that "the remains of Harry W. Prior, the light keeper of the lighthouse at Big Bay, who disappeared last June, were found by a 'land looker' Monday in the woods. The find was a gruesome one." The *Sault Ste. Marie Evening News* reported that a deer hunter discovered a human skeleton hanging by a rope from a tree limb a half mile south of Big Bay Point Lighthouse.

The lighthouse continued to be operated by a keeper until 1941, when it became automated. The lighthouse was rented out to the U.S. Army and National Guard for training purposes. In the 1950s, soldiers camped out in the meadow and woods to the west of the lighthouse.

In the summer of 1952, thirty-eight-year-old Lieutenant Coleman Peterson was temporarily stationed at Big Bay. Peterson was a veteran of the Korean War and an active member of the 768th antiaircraft battalion at Camp McCoy in Wisconsin.

One night, he walked into the Lumberjack Tavern and killed Maurice "Mike" Chenoweth. Chenoweth was the owner and bartender of the Lumberjack. Peterson shot Chenoweth because he believed the man had raped his wife, Charlotte Ann, earlier that evening. Peterson was eventually found not guilty by reason of insanity after being represented by defense attorney John D. Voelker.

The famous case was the basis for the book *Anatomy of a Murder*, written by Voelker under the pen name Robert Travers. The book became an award-winning movie starring Jimmy Stewart, George C. Scott, and Eve Arden. Many scenes from the movie were filmed in Big Bay and other cities in Michigan's Upper Peninsula.

In 1961, the lighthouse was decommissioned by the Coast Guard. Plastic surgeon Dr. John Pick purchased the structure and thirty-three acres of land for $40,000. He spent over seventeen years restoring the lighthouse but never saw his dream finalized. He sold the house to Dan Hitchens, who turned it into a corporate retreat center.

Norman and Marilyn Gotschall purchased the lighthouse in the mid-1980s and turned it into a bed-and-breakfast. They brought back the third-order Fresnel lens from the Park Place Hotel in Traverse City and displayed it in the fog signal building they restored. They purchased more land and ended up with over one hundred acres around the lighthouse.

Norman knew right away the place was haunted. His first night there was windy, and there was a loud banging that was driving him crazy. But every time he went outside to see what was loose, the wind and the banging both quit. He figured it was the keeper welcoming him to the lighthouse.

One day, a cleaning lady ran screaming up the stairs from the basement. Someone was running the shower even though no one else was down there. By the time Gotschall went to check, the water was off. Prior was the only keeper to meet a tragic end, so Gotschall figured it must be him haunting the place. Gotschall said, "Every morning in the spring he wakes me up, taps me lightly, and bids me to go fishing. I know that fishing was important to a lighthouse keeper. So I have to fish every morning. I've always tried to comply. I don't want a mad ghost around."

In March 1992, three preservationists from Chicago—John Gale and Linda and Jeff Gamble—purchased the lighthouse. Linda heard slamming cupboards in the kitchen once and realized it must have been Prior because no one else was there when she stormed in.

Nick Korstad purchased the lighthouse in 2018 and had a ghostly experience when he first bought the place. He told *Northern Express*, "It was haunted when I acquired it, there was an apartment in the basement where the previous owners had left a lot of stuff behind. I heard a lot of commotion downstairs and thought someone was in the basement. When I heard them coming up the stairs—I was in the dining room—I heard them walk into the kitchen. I looked over, and no one was there. I felt it walk up behind me, and then it went out through the front door all at once." He said, "Whatever it was, I don't know…" He never saw or felt anything like that again.

The ghost of William Prior seems to be very active. Many visitors have spotted a tall, red-headed man wearing a late 1800s uniform walking the grounds around the lighthouse. One guest was shocked to see the reflection of a man wearing a keeper's hat standing behind her when she looked in the mirror. Other guests have been awakened from a deep sleep only to find a man staring at them from the ends of their beds.

Prior is not the only spirit haunting the lighthouse; many see three souls of those lost to a shipwreck in Lake Superior. Their bodies washed up on the shore, and their spirits are said to remain around the lighthouse. There's also a story about a young woman who fell at the lighthouse and later died in Marquette sometime during the 1950s. Her spirit remains.

Guests of the bed-and-breakfast have even reported having conversations with her. For some reason, she returned to the scene of her fall and stayed.

The ghosts enjoy opening and closing doors and windows, turning lights on and off, and wandering the wooden floors, the sounds of their disembodied footsteps echoing in the old building.

CHAPTER 5

LUMBERJACKS AND LEGENDS

UNVEIL THE HAUNTING HISTORY
OF THE THUNDER BAY INN, BIG BAY

400 BENSINGER STREET, BIG BAY, MI 49808

In the heart of Big Bay, Michigan, where the wind whispers tales of lumber barons and icy winters, stands the Thunder Bay Inn, a historical haven steeped in more than just sawdust and nostalgia. Its weathered walls, built on a foundation of hand-cut stone in 1909, echo with the whispers of a bygone era when lumberjacks ruled and an unchecked temper turned into murder.

Born as a bustling general store, the Thunder Bay Inn witnessed the rise and fall of Big Bay's lumber industry. It was the heart of a lumber town acting as the general store, lumber warehouse, and first aid station. In 1944, Henry Ford became captivated by the area's raw beauty and strategic location. He purchased the building, transforming it into a personal and business retreat. The inn became a playground for Ford executives as Big Bay became a company town. Ford purchased the power plant, sawmill, and pretty much every other building in town, creating infrastructure and jobs.

After Henry Ford's passing in 1947, the Ford Motor Company lost interest in the area. By 1951, the Ford Motor Company had abandoned the venture and sold off all the properties.

Then Hollywood came knocking in 1959, choosing the inn as a backdrop for the film *Anatomy of a Murder*. The film was based on the novel of the same name written by defense attorney John D. Voelker under the

Thunder Bay Inn.

pen name Robert Travers. *Anatomy of a Murder* was a dramatization of a real murder that happened in Big Bay in 1952. Voelker was the defense attorney for Lieutenant Coleman Peterson, who shot and killed the owner and bartender of the Lumberjack Tavern because he believed the man had raped his wife.

A tavern "shell" was built for the movie to represent the Lumberjack Tavern during filming. It later became a permanent functioning fixture of the inn.

Employees and guests have reported quite a bit of paranormal activity at the inn—disembodied voices, objects moved by unseen hands, and full-body apparitions. Paranormal investigators have recorded unusually high levels of EMF (electromagnetic frequency) in several areas. Voices and odd noises have been captured on audio recording devices.

Members of Grave Paranormal stayed overnight to investigate, and they had strange spikes on their EMF, heard an odd whistle while conducting EVPs, and the REM pod went off in the middle of the night while they were sleeping. The REM pod creates its own electromagnetic field and sounds an alarm when that field is disrupted.

A most shocking ghostly visit was witnessed by the son of the inn's owner. Duke had closed for the evening and was headed back upstairs after making a sandwich in the kitchen. He glanced to the left down the hallway and froze in disbelief. The wooden baby cradle in the hallway was moving all by itself. No one else was around, and no air currents were flowing that could cause the rocker to move on its own. All the windows and doors were closed; he had just made sure of that on his nightly rounds. He figured a motherly spirit was rocking her ghost child to sleep. The presence didn't seem menacing, but he keeps his distance just to be safe.

If you crave a taste of history with a chilling twist, step into the Thunder Bay Inn.

CHAPTER 6

ECHOES OF THE IRON INDUSTRY

FAYETTE HISTORIC STATE PARK, GARDEN

4785 II ROAD, GARDEN, MI 49835

Specters of the past linger among the remnants of this iron industry town in Michigan's Upper Peninsula. The ghost town of Fayette juts between Snail Shell Harbor and Sand Bay in Big Bay de Noc. Gorgeous rock bluffs overlook the 40-acre historical town site, which is part of a much larger 850-acre state park.

In 1864, the Peninsula Railroad established a vital link between Negaunee Mine and Escanaba. This led to the development of an iron loading dock in Escanaba, transforming it into a thriving port city. This strategic location extended the shipping season and proved more economical than transporting goods across Lake Superior.

The Jackson Iron Company, an enterprise operating iron mines in Negaunee, had a particular interest in the deep waters of Snail Shell Harbor. The area was perfect for shipping iron ore; the surrounding forests had plenty of timber, which was necessary to create charcoal for iron smelting; and the land was filled with limestone, which could be quarried on-site. Limestone was another necessary ingredient to create pig iron.

In 1867, Fayette Brown, the company's agent and the town's namesake, received approval to initiate the construction of an iron smelting facility. Just two years after the conclusion of the Civil War, construction commenced in Snail Shell Harbor.

By 1869, Fayette was a bustling little town filled with various establishments such as a superintendent's house, nine frame houses, forty log houses, a town hall, a hotel, a boardinghouse, an icehouse, a meat market, an apothecary, and a doctor's office. It was very close to being a self-sustaining town. For over two decades after the Civil War, Fayette was a booming iron smelting center for the Jackson Iron Company.

Smelting operations ceased in 1891. After that, the town became a popular tourist destination and fishing village. In 1959, it became a Michigan state park.

History's soot-filled skies, shouts of iron workers, and the deafening roar of the twin blast furnaces are a stark contrast to today's serene views and the peaceful sounds of Lake Michigan lapping at the limestone shoreline. This historic location is nestled between stone cliffs, green forests, and the brilliant blue waters of Lake Michigan. Many old structures remain, including a hotel, the blast furnaces, the charcoal kilns, the town hall, a blacksmith's shop, a doctor's home and office, the superintendent's home, and many other smaller homes.

It's quite picturesque, but if you're sensitive, you can feel the tendrils of history reaching for you, ghosts that want to be remembered. Paranormal groups consider the town to be a haunted hot spot. Voices can be heard in the night, screams have been heard in the forests surrounding the town, and

Fayette, Michigan.

footsteps echo in empty buildings. There's a legend that tells of a murderous town doctor who killed himself and a patient in the forest outside town. The legend says these poor souls still wander through the forest at night.

The old blast furnaces are filled with spirits. Not surprising, as that's the location where so many men were injured or killed. Several of the old homes have that "feeling." They may look empty, but the past is there. If you squint just right, you might catch a glimpse of the wraiths that walk between realms.

The old hotel doesn't check in guests anymore. It sits as an empty reminder of the past, filled with Plexiglas-entombed exhibits to give you an idea of what life was like in the town's heyday. However, you can camp at the park's modern campground or moor your boat in one of the slip rentals. History and nature blend in this beautiful state park. You can learn about the past, hike the trails, swim at the beach, or boat the clear blue waters. There are two beaches—the slag beach at the historic town site and a swimming beach that is just a short hike from the campground through the woods.

South of the town site are the ruins of a church and the old fishermen cemetery. The cemetery is near the public beach parking area overlooking the bay.

The first Saturday in October, the Fayette campground usually has a Fall Fest filled with Halloween fun, including hay rides and a haunted trail. The historic site occasionally hosts paranormal events and ghost hunts.

The state park is open daily all year round from 8:00 a.m. to 10:00 p.m. The park's historic town site buildings and campgrounds are only open from mid-May to mid-October. The boat slips are available to rent from early May to early November. To access the park, visitors will need a current Michigan Recreational Passport.

PART II
MICHIGAN'S ISLAND OF THE DEAD

Porch.com named Mackinac Island America's Most Haunted City: "Topping the torrid table of the most haunted towns is Mackinac Island, MI. Its excruciatingly high ratio of 16 haunted sites per 478 people makes it the most haunted small town in America." Porch.com used data from the Shadowlands Haunted Places Index to discover the scariest sites and states in the United States. This island of the dead is home to many ghosts.

Amy Bruni, one of the stars of *Ghost Hunters*, believes that Mackinac Island's hauntings have a lot to do with how it still remains much the same as it did in the Victorian era. Frozen in history while existing in the present, Mackinac Island is a liminal space.

"Mackinac is legitimately a step back in time," she said. "They don't allow motorized vehicles on the island, so it's so quiet and you just feel like you're from another era. They have also put a huge focus on restoration and preservation—so, it puts you in the mindset that you can connect more with any spirits that may be lingering. You're looking at the island exactly as they did—and I think that's why so many never leave. It's always the same."

Mackinac was sacred to the Anishnaabek. It was a place where they buried their dead and performed ceremonies to honor their ancestors and Gitche Manitou, the Great Spirit. Seventeenth-century French explorers and Jesuit priests described the ceremonies as "feasts of the dead." This ceremony is still practiced by some Native communities in Michigan. They call them Ghost Suppers.

The Anishnaabek say the "island is their place of origin, where they've always been and still, in many cases, reside near

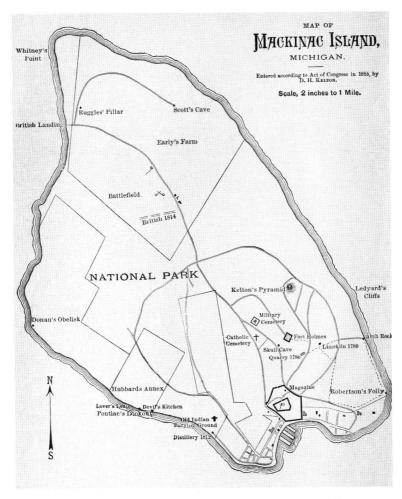

A map of Mackinac Island in the front matter of the book *Annals of Fort Mackinac*, 1889.

and around." Research indicates Native Americans inhabited the island as far back as AD 900. Some of the Native burials were moved to tribal lands, but many remain on the island.

The Anishnaabek named the island Michilimackinac, which translates to "Great Turtle." If you visit by ferry, watch as the island appears. It looks like a turtle rising out of the water. When you're in the straits, also be on the lookout for the ghost ships the *Griffon* and the *W.H. Gilcher*. You may even catch sight of the sea serpent that lives in the waters.

The first white man known to visit Mackinac Island was a French Canadian fur trader named Jean Nicolet in 1634. In 1670, the island became a hub for fur trading. After the French and Indian War, the British took the Straits of Mackinac and built Fort Mackinac on the bluffs in 1780. Three years later, the Americans took the fort when it was given to them in a treaty after the Revolution. During the War of 1812, the British fought to take back the island.

In July 1812, the British snuck onto the island in an area now called British Landing and forced the Americans to surrender. They brutally murdered seventy-five Native men. Many have seen the spirits of these men running through the woods to escape the slaughter at the shore. By 1814, the Americans tried to retake the island but had to fight combined forces of British, Canadian, and Native soldiers. A plaque now marks the spot where this battle took place. Ghosts also mark the spot and are often seen and heard in this location. The fort remained active until 1895, but the island had become quite a tourist location by that point.

Records prior to the 1800s showcase burial locations of American and British soldiers, civilians, and Native Americans. Three cemeteries were relocated when the island started becoming more populated: St. Anne's, the Post Cemetery, and Mackinac Island Cemetery. Numerous Native American graves have been discovered during excavations at Skull Cave, Marquette Park, the Grand Hotel, and Haan's 1830 Inn.

After the federal government turned the island over to the State of Michigan, it was turned into Michigan's first state park, which encompasses approximately 80 percent of the island. In 1898, vehicles were banned from the island. This ban remains in effect today. To get around on Mackinac Island, you walk, take a horse-drawn carriage, or ride a bicycle.

Many of the hotels on the island are rumored to be haunted.

CHAPTER 7

UNEARTHING SECRETS AT THE GRAND HOTEL, MACKINAC ISLAND

286 GRAND AVENUE, MACKINAC ISLAND, MI 49757

The Grand Hotel first opened on July 10, 1887, and is reportedly one of the most haunted spots on the island. It has the standard haunts—ghostly footsteps, doors that open and close by themselves—but it also has apparitions, including soldiers that wander the halls and Victorian-clad adults and children who drift through the employee housing. Little "Rebecca" floats down hallways on the fourth floor. A man with a top hat appears to guests in the piano bar before disappearing in a puff of cigar smoke, while a Victorian-clad woman likes to snuggle in next to employees when they go

Grand Hotel, Mackinac Island.

to bed at night. And on the world's longest porch, a ghostly woman in black can sometimes be spotted walking her large white dog.

Then there's the demon of the Grand Hotel. Two maintenance men had a run-in with a black, red-eyed shadowy mass on the theater stage. The mass rushed one man, knocking him to the floor. The man woke up two days later in the hospital and has never returned to the hotel.

The Grand Hotel does not like to talk about paranormal activity, though occasionally you can get a chatty bellhop who will regale you with tales of full-body apparitions.

Post Cemetery was moved to make room for the hotel's stables, but were all the bodies moved? Old stories say that skeletal remains were found numerous times during construction, not just in the area of the stable but all over the grounds of the Grand Hotel. Workers finally stopped moving them and just built the hotel over the bones.

CHAPTER 8
ECHOES OF THE PAST

MISSION POINT RESORT'S HAUNTING HISTORY, MACKINAC ISLAND

1 LAKESHORE DRIVE, MACKINAC ISLAND, MI 49757

Mission Point is a hot spot of paranormal activity on the island. It started as a fishing camp for Native tribes and later was claimed by British captain Daniel Robertson in 1782. He built a small home at the location to entertain guests and military personnel. The story says it was built too close to the cliff and fell over. As the legend was retold over and over, the name was switched to Robinson and the house became Robinson's Folly.

A young minister named Reverend William Montague Ferry stepped onto the island in 1823. In 1825, he opened Mission House School, giving Mission Point its name. The three-story wood-framed Mission House still stands today. It is on both the Michigan and National Register of Historic Places. This mission was constructed to serve as a place for the American Board of Commissioners for Foreign Missions to enlighten the Native Americans about Christianity. It is said that tribal people willingly sent their children to Mission Point. Unlike later boarding schools that forced tribal children to attend and prohibited the speaking of Native languages, the Mission did not strip children of their culture. They translated materials into the Native language. The school taught English and other subjects. It housed around five hundred Native American and Métis children. There were sixteen known deaths among the students due to illness. Those poor children are thought to be the spirits haunting Mission House, which now is home to seasonal island employees. The ghostly children wander the first

GENERAL VIEW OF HARBOR, OLD MISSION POINT AND FORT, MACKINAC ISLAND, MICH.— 28

Old Mission Point.

two floors and the basement. They have been known to bounce balls and knock over alarm clocks.

Around 1830, the Mission Point Church was built. In the mid-1830s, Reverend Ferry and his family left the island. The school sat empty until the 1840s, when Edward and Mary Frank purchased the property. They added a third floor to the school building and opened it as a hotel. The Mission Hotel was operated for over ninety years by the family until the Great Depression forced them to close their doors.

In the 1940s, Dr. Frank Buchman's ideals were gaining traction. The Moral Re-Armament (MRA), a religious organization (cult), had some big-name followers, like Henry Ford. In 1942, Buchman was staying with the Fords and happened to mention he was looking for a place to hold his summer convention. Clara Ford suggested Mackinac Island. Buchman was more than interested, especially when he learned the price. Clara Ford worked out a deal with the Michigan governor so the MRA could rent the Mission Point Hotel and land for one dollar a year.

In 1955, Mission Point was remodeled into a conference center and became the worldwide headquarters for the MRA. Over the next ten years, they built nine structures, including a large theater and soundstage where they produced major motion pictures as propaganda to promote a "theater of hope presenting what society could be." When it was finished, they had orchestra rehearsal rooms, two major soundstages, set design, and construction shops. It was the second-largest television studio in America at the time. The theater was later used as a major filming site for the 1980 film *Somewhere in Time*, starring Christopher Reeve and Jane Seymour.

In 1960, Frances Lacey of Dearborn, Michigan, was staying at what is now the Murray Hotel. She went missing on Sunday, July 24, 1960. Her body was found five days later on the property of the Moral Re-Armament Organization. Her murder remains unsolved. Some say her spirit wanders the island, most often seen on the grounds of Mission Point, though sometimes she is seen at the Murray.

In 1966, the location became Mackinac College, but only one class graduated. The school had terrible financial difficulties, and after just three years, it was going to close, but the staff stayed, many working for free for a fourth year so that one class could graduate.

In February 1967, a horrible tragedy occurred when a student committed suicide, reportedly after his girlfriend said no to his marriage proposal. Heartbroken "Harvey" grabbed a shotgun, went into the woods behind campus, and shot himself. This occurred in February, but his body was not found until July. He had two shotgun wounds in his head. All the tales told say there was no gun found with him. Rumors swirled that Harvey's girlfriend said no to the proposal because she already had another man, and

Mackinac Island, Mich.   248 Old Mission House

MANUFACTURED BY CURT TEICH & CO., CHICAGO, ILL.

Mission House.

that man killed Harvey. The official cause of death was listed as suicide. But how do you shoot yourself in the head twice with a shotgun?

Old newspaper reports from July 20, 1967, state that the nineteen-year-old college freshman's body was found in a densely wooded area with a gun next to it. There was no mention of him being jilted by a lover. It took six months to find him, which is not surprising with how cold and frozen Mackinac is in winter. But what is odd is that the search was called off because a classmate received a letter from Harvey stating that he was dropping out of school but planned to stay on the island. Also odd—his parents were vacationing on the island when his body was found. What?

"Harvey" is not his real name, but his parents requested that his name not be associated with ghost stories.

Legend has it that Harvey haunts Mission Point, flirting with female guests in hopes of finding true love, even in his afterlife, though his methods are not garnering much affection. Female theater visitors are often pinched and poked by unseen hands. Harvey also likes to turn off lights and slam doors. He has been spotted on the bluffs behind the resort.

Television evangelist Rex Humbard turned Mission Point into a Christian college with 171 students in 1971. Humbard purchased quite a bit of land on the island to create a ski resort and a ski team for the college. But financial problems shut everything down after only a year.

The luxurious Mission Point Resort has been open since the early 1970s. It has changed owners and names over the years. The Inn on Mackinac was its name during the filming of *Somewhere in Time* during the summer of 1979.

In the 1980s, a front desk supervisor was walking down a hallway while closing the resort for the season. Suddenly, all of the doors behind him slammed shut.

Many shadowy figures roam the hallways and rooms of the resort, while apparitions of soldiers and Native Americans are often spotted on the grounds. Shadow people and terrifying doppelgangers have also been seen. An ethereal little girl named Lucy continually searches for her parents, while a ghostly woman hums and sings in the theater. Shadows and voices drift through the theater continuously. The dressing rooms are creepy, cramped, and filled with paranormal activity. One investigation caught a voice—possibly the spirit of a diva actress—telling everyone to "get out" of her dressing room.

In July 2020, *Haunted Detroit* author Nicole Beauchamp was investigating Strait's Lodge conference center at Mission Point. The building was empty other than Nicole and her cousin Lauren, but they kept hearing noises in the restroom like someone was in there moving around. Inside the meeting room, they spotted a fuzzy shadow figure that stood out from the darkness. Trying to communicate, they knocked a pattern on the wall, and something knocked back, completing the pattern.

The SyFy Channel's popular show *Ghost Hunters* filmed season 7, episode 6 at Mission Point. The episode, titled "Frozen in Fear," first aired on March 30, 2011. Room 2200 in Strait's Lodge is one of the most active spots in the resort. Maria Holt-Aistrop has conducted investigations in the room that turned up quite a bit of evidence, from EVP to being touched by unseen hands. One woman had to leave the room because a red handprint appeared on her skin. Shadow figures and disembodied voices are the most common disturbances reported in room 2200. Other investigators at Mission Point have picked up EVP of the words "shotgun," "soundstage," "mommy," and "daddy."

On the Mission Point property, a large natural pond formed between the putting greens of the eighteen-hole golf course and the rough shoreline of Lake Huron. Numerous people have reported seeing dark shapes, shadowy figures, and apparitions near this pond, which has been dubbed the Drowning Pool.

Many rumors have been spread about witches, brothels, and drownings in this pool. Paranormal researcher Todd Clements is referenced on countless websites and articles stating that "back in the 1700s and early 1800s when Fort Mackinac was at its heyday, a lot of brothels popped up. Seven women were accused of being witches and enticing unsuspecting soldiers, fur traders, and husbands to their houses. It is said that rocks were tied around their ankles and they were thrown into the lagoon."

CHAPTER 9

WHISPERS IN THE PINES

UNRAVELING THE SECRETS OF PINE COTTAGE, MACKINAC ISLAND

1427 BOGAN LANE, MACKINAC ISLAND, MI 49757

Built in 1870, Pine Cottage was one of the first Mackinac Island hotels to be established. It is said that famous guests like Ty Cobb and Ernest Hemingway have stayed there.

The ghosts most often seen are a woman, a man, and a young girl. One of the cottage ghost stories involves a young girl who lived there with her alcoholic parents. The parents moved and left the young girl alone. She died at the cottage, but her spirit never left. Another story involves a woman who was brutally murdered in the cottage by a large man in 1942. There are no news reports of murder on Mackinac other than the 1960 murder of Frances Lacey. Perhaps the story was made up to thrill tourists.

When Bob Hughey bought the house, he claimed that a spirit made herself known with ghostly footsteps and moving objects. But then one day, half a specter rushed out of the closet and ran right at Bob. The ghost moved right through him and then disappeared out the window. After that manifestation, shadow figures started appearing. The sad-faced little blonde girl is the spirit most often spotted. She stares out a window, crying inconsolably.

The scariest thing anyone has seen is called the "creature"—a hunchback man with horns sprouting from his spine. The Hugheys moved to St. Ignace in the 1990s. The B&B still gets reports of haunting and strange activity.

A friendlier ghost greets guests at another island hotel that wishes to remain unnamed. A kindly old gentleman named Charlie can usually be found on the fourth floor in rooms 400 and 409. He likes to play with water. He often turns on the showers and hot tubs. He also messes up electronics, turns lights on and off, and rearranges furniture. The Michigan Area Paranormal Investigation Team gathered quite a bit of evidence about the spirit named Charlie, including a photo of what appears to be a ghostly man, five feet, six inches, in a jacket and top hat.

CHAPTER 10
GHOSTLY GUESTS AND ISLAND LEGENDS

TALES OF THE PARANORMAL FROM MACKINAC'S HOTELS

Numerous other hotels, inns, and bed-and-breakfasts on the island have haunting tales attached to them, possibly due to their age, history, and the active imaginations of islanders.

THE INN AT STONECLIFFE

8593 CUDAHY CIRCLE, MACKINAC ISLAND, MI 49757

The Inn at Stonecliffe was built by businessman Michael Cudahy in 1904. He had it designed by architect Frederick Perkins, who also designed the Governor's Island Cottage. In 1966, the property was sold to the Moral Re-Armament Movement, which used the property as a retreat for high-level members. In 1972, it was turned into a ski resort. Over the years, it has changed hands numerous times. It's now a beautifully renovated resort getaway thought to be haunted by at least one ghostly servant girl from the past. The girl is thought to have been a servant to the original owners, the Cudahy family, and is often seen on the third floor in or near the area of the original servant quarters. Furniture in the area often is moved without explanation, and some claim to have caught the apparition on camera. One night she even spooked a few horses on their way into Stonecliffe.

BOGAN LANE INN

1420 Bogan Lane, Mackinac Island, MI 49757

Bogan Lane was built in the 1850s as a single-family residence when the Mackinac fishing industry was expanding. Many of the families that developed the fishing industry in the area were immigrants from Ireland during the potato famine.

After the fishing industry's boom era, the home sat vacant for over forty years. In 1957, a new foundation, bathrooms, and a heating system were installed.

Now, the quant inn is open year-round. Its bright, beautiful spaces make it hard to believe anything scary goes on there, but some have reported a little ghost girl haunts the place. She's been spotted playing the piano and often tells guests she wants to go home.

In October 2019, a guest reported that they couldn't sleep well. Each of their two nights, they were awakened by the sound of their doorknob rattling and turning like someone was going to open the door any second.

Another guest reported that their TV flickered constantly. So a new TV was placed in their room. It had worked fine in a different room, but this second TV also flickered. They spoke to a little girl who was a guest at the same time they were, and the girl said the inn was haunted and the ghost girl was her friend.

MÉTIVIER INN

7466 Market Street, Mackinac Island, MI 49757

In 1877, Civil War veteran Louis Joseph Métivier purchased a Victorian home that would become the Métivier Inn one hundred years later. For years, Josephine, Louis's wife, rented out rooms, and later their daughter Mabel ran the house as a dormitory for college-age island employees.

The home stayed in the Métivier family until 1985, when new owners turned it into a bed-and-breakfast.

It is said that a kindly spirit haunts the house, "just checking" on guests before disappearing.

HARBOUR VIEW INN

6860 Main Street, Mackinac Island, MI 49757

Magdelaine Marcotte was born in 1780 to a French Canadian fur trader and a Native woman who was the daughter of Odawa (Ottawa) Chief Kewanoquat. In 1794, Magdelaine married prominent businessman Joseph L. Framboise in a traditional Ottawa marriage ceremony. They settled on Mackinac Island and were remarried in 1804 in St. Anne's Church. Magdelaine's close connection to the church played a significant role throughout her life and death.

Joseph was murdered in 1806, and instead of selling off his businesses, Magdelaine decided to run them herself. She made quite a name for herself as a businesswoman. Her daughter Josette married Fort Mackinac commander Captain Benjamin Pierce, brother to future president Franklin Pierce. Captain Pierce built Madame La Framboise a beautiful home that is now the Harbor View Inn. Unfortunately, Josette died in childbirth to her second child, Langdon, who passed shortly after. When Magdelaine passed, she joined her daughter Josette and grandson Langdon, who were buried under the altar of the new St. Anne's Church, which Magdelaine had donated land for, across the street from her home, Harbor View.

In the 1950s, St. Anne's decided to build a basement, which required them to move the bodies of the La Framboise family. It is said their remains were stored in a barn for several years before being properly buried in the churchyard.

And that's where the haunting stories begin. Magdelaine's house and tombstone have been reported to "glow" in photographs with an unearthly light, as if the stone was on fire surrounded by yellow, red, and orange lights. The church basement was plagued by slumping walls and cracked plaster due to a curse thought to have been placed by Magdelaine herself. The spirit of Madame La Framboise is said to still walk the halls of her beautiful home. Photos and videos of her former bedroom often end up blank or heavily distorted.

For an incredible book detailing the life of Madame La Framboise, check out *Ardent Spirit: Based on the True Story of Magdelaine La Framboise.*

PART III
HAVE SPIRITS WILL TRAVEL
NORTHWEST MICHIGAN

Northwest Michigan is at the Tip of the Mitt. It's a picturesque region characterized by its stunning landscapes, outdoor recreational opportunities, and charming communities.

Traverse City is the largest city in the region, known for its Cherry Festival, a vibrant downtown area, cultural events, and many wineries. Petoskey is known for its Victorian architecture and arts scene. It's also near the scenic Tunnel of Trees, which is a popular destination in the autumn for those who love to see the fall colors.

Northwest Michigan is filled with ghost stories. Tales of spectral activity abound at the Weathervane Restaurant in Charlevoix, City Park Grill in Petoskey, Bowers Harbor Inn on Old Mission Peninsula, and the Ramsdell Theatre in Manistee.

CHAPTER 11

VICTORIAN ELEGANCE AND SPOOKY SPECTERS

THE TERRACE INN, PETOSKEY

1549 GLENDALE AVENUE, PETOSKEY, MI 49770

The beautiful lakeside town of Petoskey has been a popular summer retreat since the mid-1870s. A few famous visitors include Helen Keller, Booker T. Washington, and Ernest Hemingway.

The Bay View Association was established in 1875, and its headquarters is now a National Historical Landmark. If you love Victorian architecture, you'll be in for a treat driving through this area. The association includes 445 "cottages," many of which are grand Victorians. Some of the cottages have spectacular views of Lake Michigan.

The Petoskey area emits an aura tinged with history and permeated with the energy of the great lake. Power and beauty collide in this lakeside city.

The Terrace Inn is filled with Victorian luxury—hardwood floors, crystal chandeliers, and wrought-iron bed frames. Stare hard enough and you might see the ghosts of the past dining in the magnificent dining room. The inn is one of the most active haunts in Michigan.

The Terrace Inn dates back to the early 1900s. William J. Devol was a prominent businessman from Indiana. He vacationed with his wife and three daughters in Bay View every summer. He decided the area needed a good hotel and took ownership of the old Terrace Inn, which had been damaged by fire. In 1911, renovations were completed, and the new Terrace Inn opened its doors. Happiness and tragedy have mingled throughout the

Terrace Inn dining room.

years, but the ghostly shenanigans seem to have started in the 1970s, when major renovations began.

When Patty and Mo Rave purchased the inn in 2004, they were handed the ghost files along with keys. The three-ring binder contained all the accounts of spooky occurrences guests have experienced at the inn throughout the decades.

Why is the place so haunted?

The Terrace Inn, 1911.

There are a couple of stories of deaths at the inn. Two workers were killed during the 1910 reconstruction, and their spirits can sometimes be seen wandering the property. Psychics have picked up on the energy of someone jumping out of an upper window, fleeing for their life. Perhaps during a fire or accident? The Red Cross used the inn as a hospital during World War I. It was referred to as the House Hospital.

There is a ghostly urban legend that a lady in white continually searches for her husband, Edward, who can occasionally be spotted dressed in tweed. The two spirits are never seen together but seem to be searching for each other. Guests have spotted a woman in a white Victorian dress on the third floor and heard a woman's voice calling for Edward. It is believed that the woman's spirit is Elizabeth Abby Sweet. She was pregnant with twins when she visited the inn. She fell, and neither she nor her twins survived the fall. Years later, her husband, Edward, is said to have returned to the inn, where he died of a broken heart. Supposedly, Elizabeth passed away in room 211 and Edward passed in room 308. Both rooms have numerous haunting tales tied to them.

The second floor is where most of the spectral activity occurs. Two rooms get reported quite often: 211 and 212.

In the winter of 2005, a guest named Francie was staying in room 212. It was the off-season, so she was the only guest in that area of the inn. At

3:00 a.m., she was rudely awakened by a woman talking and laughing very loudly outside her door. She seemed to be telling her friends goodnight before slamming her door shut. At first, Francie thought it was just another guest being rude, but then remembered she was alone in that area of the inn. She tried to go back to sleep, but forty minutes later, the entire situation repeated. Francie couldn't go back to sleep. She looked out her door and found the hallway empty and all the doors open, just as they had been when she went to bed. The same exact scenario happened to a guest named Paddy who stayed in room 212 in March 2005.

One guest from October 2015 reported feeling an overwhelming sense of sadness as soon as they entered the room. They felt inconsolable, like crying the entire time they were in the room.

Room 212 has quite a few reports of a ghost light. The room will be completely dark, and then suddenly it's like someone turned on a light, though no one in the room did.

Room 211 is considered to be the heart of the haunt. Visitors have said the air feels thick and tense. A woman's angry energy is felt. Perhaps Elizabeth is angry that she fell and died. Or is she angry at someone who caused her fall?

In room 211, guests have experienced waking up to the spectral sound of a woman singing, ghostly hangers clanking in the closet even though the actual hangers are filled with clothing and would not clank, and the odd scent of very old cologne permeating the space. Guests have also awakened to curtains wide open in the morning even though they went to sleep with them closed.

In 2011, a guest named Kenneth reported that the door would not stay closed even though he shut and locked it. After dinner, he came back to find the door wide open. When he got into bed, it sounded like someone was knocking on the door, but no one was there. Throughout the night, the door opened three times, even though he had locked it tight.

Several guests have reported experiencing a weird form of sleep paralysis in room 211. The creepiest occurrence happened to a guest named Laura in 2013. "It was around midnight, and I had finally fallen asleep, or so I thought. I felt something crawl under the covers with me. It entered the covers at my neck and continued down to my stomach. The feeling was electrically charged—almost a tingling feeling. I opened my eyes and tried to scream, but I couldn't. Something screamed in my face. My heart was pounding. I lay in bed petrified; every hair on my body stood on end."

In January 2015, Anthony and Rebecca stayed in room 211. The night started with Anthony feeling something touch his back. Rebecca spotted a weird black mist at the end of the bed. During the night, Anthony was dreaming of a woman lying on top of him and woke up to actual pressure on his body like someone was lying on him. He started to doze back off when a man's voice said, "How is he able to go back to sleep now?" right in his ear. Terrified, he woke up Rebecca and shared his story.

Room 205 has had numerous reports of ghostly whispering and voices in the night. Another guest named Rebecca stayed in 2014 and was awakened by the feeling of something touching her toes. After waking fully, she heard whispering, a man and a woman talking in hushed tones. The next night, the same couple was heard talking outside the room. When she looked, no one was in the hall or any of the rooms.

The third floor is filled with strange noises, bodiless footsteps, orbs, and shadow men. Many have spotted a shadowy figure on the stairs; a few have even heard him speak. A shadow man and a ghostly child have been seen numerous times throughout the inn.

Other hauntings include hushed whispers of a woman speaking in old-fashioned English. Objects move by themselves, and alarm clocks and lights turn on and off by themselves. The presence of a young male no older than thirteen or fourteen has been sensed by numerous researchers. One night, a group of women was sitting inside the inn talking when the piano behind them started playing on its own. Numerous paranormal investigators have caught EVPs and EMF readings throughout the inn.

The Terrace Inn, 2023.

Several EVPs were recorded in the dining room. In March 2007, a male voice was recorded saying the name "Abby Sweet." Authors Kat Tedsen and Bev Rydel found evidence of Abby Sweet, who emigrated from Ireland to New York in the early 1900s to marry. Her last letter to family indicated that she was traveling to northern Michigan to be a maid at a new luxury hotel. She was never heard from again. Could this be Elizabeth Sweet?

Former night manager Angie would often spot a white Victorian gown floating in the laundry room. Sometimes she would see it out of the corner of her eye, other times right in front of her—just a dress, floating in midair, that would slowly fade away. She never felt threatened by it. The presence felt comforting, like a mother watching over a child. This was completely different than the vibes she got from the kitchen and dry storage room in the basement. Employees hated going into the dry storage room. The sounds of breaking glass were often accompanied by a feeling of menace.

If you happen to spot a spirit at the inn, be sure to add your account to the ghost file at the front desk. Patty and Mo were always open to paranormal researchers and even hosted the Little Traverse Bay ParaFest at the Terrace.

Patty and Mo sold the Terrace in July 2023 to Marybeth Bennett.

CHAPTER 12

UNEXPLAINED ENCOUNTERS AT STAFFORD'S PERRY HOTEL, PETOSKEY

100 LEWIS STREET, PETOSKEY, MI 49770

The village of Petoskey was settled in 1879. It's a quiet town and a popular tourist destination, especially for rock hunters looking for Petoskey stones, after which the village was named. The peculiar state stone is a type of fossilized coral found abundantly in the area. Dr. Norman J. Perry gave up his dental practice in 1899 and decided to build the Perry Hotel at the corner of Bay and Lewis Streets. This prime location overlooks Little Traverse Bay along Michigan's Gold Coast. In 1916, Ernest Hemingway hiked and camped his way to northern Michigan with a friend. When he arrived in Petoskey, Hemingway stayed at the Perry Hotel. A commemorative plaque notes this as part of a series of Hemingway's Michigan Historical Markers.

Norman Perry operated the hotel for twenty years before selling it. The hotel flourished under the management of D. Herbert Reycraft, who transformed the Perry into a tourist destination. He expanded, adding a four-story, forty-six-room wing in 1926. The Perry is a central part of Petoskey's history and connected to many tales in the area, including stories of hauntings.

Stafford's Perry Hotel has many specters roaming the halls. On the third floor, Doris haunts the library. Room 310 is very active; many guests and staff members have reported something strange about that room. A ghostly custodian named Keith still wanders around, keeping an eye on the place, and a little girl plays in the restaurant and enjoys scaring the staff.

Hotel Perry.

Stafford's Perry Hotel.

One night, a manager was closing up during the Winter Blues Festival. Balloons were tied to all the chairs in the dining room. The manager had just turned out the lights when he heard a loud *pop* and the pitter-patter of little feet running across the floor. Another staff member encountered a little girl sitting in a hallway chair. The staff member asked the girl if she was all right. The little girl didn't answer, so the employee kept going down the hall but glanced back just a second later, and no girl was anywhere to be seen.

A bar located in the basement, called the Noggin Room, is a hotbed of activity. Numerous accounts of glasses breaking on their own and forks flying through the air have been reported. Several people have reported the feeling of being squeezed by tiny hands underneath a table, like a child playing, being silly and grabbing people. Only there is no child there—though a little girl with golden curls has been spotted in the hotel numerous times. She peers out the library window and mysteriously shows up in photographs, but when employees check, there is never a little girl staying at the hotel. In one photo, she was standing next to a Christmas tree, though the woman who snapped the picture saw no girl there when the photo was taken. Tiny handprints appear on a large mirror in the lobby. The mirror is thirteen feet up on the wall—not an easy place for tiny fingers to reach.

Other strange occurrences include dark mists floating through rooms, an apparition of a man in a blue suit with no legs, a red book that strangely appears and disappears all over the hotel, and objects that move all by themselves.

The hotel doesn't advertise its spooky residents, but if you talk to the right staff member, you're sure to hear plenty of haunting tales.

CHAPTER 13

WANDERING SPIRITS AT THE BLUE PELICAN, CENTRAL LAKE MICHIGAN

2535 Main Street, Central Lake, MI 49622

In June 1922, fishing enthusiast L. Van Skiver posted an advertisement in the *Detroit Free Press* offering a five-dollar reward to the person who came up with the best name for a fishing resort. He built his retreat in the charming village of Central Lake, which is approximately forty miles north of Traverse City. It was built in 1924 by stonemasons Art Carpenter, Joe Blakely, and Jack Garrison. It was called We-Go-Ta. It became a popular stop for traveling salesmen and fishermen.

By 1926, ads were appearing in newspapers advertising twenty rooms and a dining capacity of one hundred. Fishers were lured in with the promise of a lake filled with trout, bass, and muskallonge.

The hotel's name was changed to Central Lake Hotel. The owner of the Central Lake Canning Company, Emmons Butler "E.B." Gill, became friends with Van Skiver. Eventually, he and his wife, Helen Mary "Nellie" Gill, moved into the hotel and began assisting with operations.

Central Lake High School caught fire in February 1927, leaving the students with no school. There were no other buildings in the area that could be used as a makeshift school, so the hotel was offered as a replacement. It filled in as the local school until a new one could be built. In 1930, Van Skiver added a tavern to the property, which drew in travelers and gave the business a steady stream of income.

Hotel We-Go-Ta.

E.B. Gill passed away in February 1943. Heartsick with grief, Nellie left the hotel for several years, but she eventually returned to the place she loved so much. She passed away on March 16, 1951, in the basement of the Central Lake Hotel.

Over the years, the hotel changed hands and names numerous times. In the 1960s, it became the Palace, and in the 1970s, it became known as the Lamplight Inn. In 1986, it became Murphy's Lamplight Inn to honor the new owners, Mike and Mary Ellen Murphy.

Chris and Merrie Corbet opened the Blue Pelican Restaurant in 2003, named after Chris's favorite restaurant in Virginia, the Blue Pelican Seafood Company. Sadly, the Blue Pelican went up in flames in July 2008. Soon after the fire, the Corbets inquired about purchasing the historic hotel, which had gone into foreclosure. By October, the hotel was theirs and they named it The Blue Pelican Inn. Chris was able to salvage his blue pelican neon sign from his restaurant and hang it in the Inn.

Chris didn't believe in ghost stories until he started experiencing things himself. Soon after moving in, neighbors began to ask about the girl in the attic window. He had no idea what they were talking about. He would encounter strange electrical currents in certain areas of the hotel. His dog would obsessively watch over him while he was in several of the rooms.

One day, a bartender was standing outside smoking a cigarette and caught movement in the upstairs window. As he looked closer, he made out the face

The Blue Pelican.

of a little girl staring back at him. When workers went to investigate, they realized the window was covered. A wall and shower had been built over it.

Investigators speculate that the girl may have been a student who died in the fire and followed her classmates to the new school, or she came to the building with something from the original school. A little girl has also been seen in the basement. She loves to sing; sometimes you can hear her songs echoing in empty hallways. In September 2023, a male child spirit was seen in the large pine tree in front of the patio portion of the restaurant.

The location has quite a few reports of odd noises—banging, scratching, tapping, and other muffled sounds that no one can seem to find a source for. Something odd happens on the stairs, usually halfway up. Quite a few people have reported "feeling" something is not quite right. Many have said they felt a sudden sense of unease, the hair rising on their neck, chills, and the sensation of being watched. Paranormal investigators have recorded EMF spikes at that exact spot on the stairs.

Workers and guests have reported seeing faces peering out of empty rooms. A couple of the spirits have possibly been identified. One is thought to be a guest from the hotel's time as a boardinghouse or possibly the daughter of one of the hotel's managers. The story goes that she was climbing down from a second-story balcony to elope with her fiancé when she tripped on the hem of her dress and fell to her death. Many have seen her sadly wandering the upstairs hallway in a white dress, while others report seeing a strange cloud of white mist floating through the halls. She's also been spotted by the entrance and climbing down from the roof. Her appearance can be very startling because her pretty white dress is covered in blood.

Another apparition that has been spotted is a man in a tuxedo. He has been seen in the bar enjoying a glass of booze, only to vanish while you are looking straight at him. One employee held the door open for him and then proceeded to get strange looks from everyone else because she was the only one who had seen him.

Mrs. Gill's ghost remains in the building. Shortly after her death in 1951, staff members started reporting spectral activity. Mrs. Gill is often spotted in the saloon and the saloon's restroom. This is the area that was once the basement where she took her last breath. Female guests have reported odd things from their visits to the restroom, including sighs, groans, and the voice of an elderly woman in the middle stall even though when they look, no one is there. One guest ran out of the bathroom screaming in fright.

Some think the hauntings are due to the "ghost closet" that contains artifacts from the hotel's history.

Currently, the Pelican has seven available guest rooms. The Cherry Room is reported to be the most haunted.

CHAPTER 14

HISTORY, HEALING, AND HAUNTING AT THE VILLAGE AT GRAND TRAVERSE COMMONS, TRAVERSE CITY

1200 WEST ELEVENTH STREET, TRAVERSE CITY, MI 49684

On November 30, 1885, the Traverse City State Hospital opened under the direction of Dr. James Decker Munson. It was designed as a place of healing and was meant to catch the overflow from the overly crowded institutions in Pontiac and Kalamazoo. Architect George Lloyd designed the asylum using the Kirkbride model. Between 1845 and 1910, a total of seventy-three Kirkbride hospitals were constructed in the United States.

The elaborate design featured a labyrinth of tunnels underground for the pipes to run through. These tunnels were a great way for staff and patients to get from one building to another without going outside in harsh weather. The sidewalks were built right on top of the tunnels so the steam from the pipes would melt the snow.

Barbaric treatments such as electroshock therapy were prohibited. Straightjackets were not allowed. This was unheard of at the time when standard practices seemed like torture compared to today's medical services. Dr. Munson was a visionary. He believed in the Kirkbride idea that "beauty is therapy." He said patients could heal better in a place of beauty and tranquility.

Patients were free to roam the well-maintained grounds and use the numerous hiking trails. The dining hall was decorated with white table linens, china place settings, and vases of freshly cut flowers. By all accounts, patients during Munson's time were treated quite well.

STATE HOSPITAL, TRAVERSE CITY, MICH.

Traverse City State Hospital.

Creativity and purpose were encouraged. The asylum residents could take part in sports and creative outlets like band and theater, and they could work. The hospital was located on 135 acres of land with a working farm, which included dairy cows and many gardens and greenhouses. Patients were allowed to work the land and farm, which was meant to help them maintain a sense of purpose while hospitalized. On Monday nights, residents were treated to a movie, and once a month, a dance was held. This social event was the only time male and female residents mingled.

The hospital also became a location for nurses to train while "on the job." Nurse Jennie A. Leese came up with the idea for the nurses training for the program, and Dr. Munson fully supported her nontraditional approach. The program continued for decades, even after Leese left.

Throughout the years, the hospital had many names as it changed and expanded to accommodate more than just mental patients. Numerous housing cottages and outbuildings were added to the grounds. The Northern Michigan Asylum, Traverse City Regional Psychiatric Hospital, and the Northern Michigan State Hospital were a few of the names it had over the years. Those with diseases such as typhoid, polio, and influenza were welcomed. Later, it was used as a drug rehabilitation center and then a home for the elderly. But of course, budgets were eventually cut and funding slashed.

Willow Lake.

After 104 years of service, the hospital closed its doors in 1989. Over two hundred jobs were lost when the hospital closed, and many of the patients were left with nowhere to go. Some wandered off and lived in the surrounding woods. But few survived the harsh Michigan winters.

Even though the place was designed to be beautiful and tranquil, stories of hauntings and dark spirits abound. As with any institution, there are stories of employees taking advantage of patients, abusing them, and doing unspeakable things to those in their care. Such trauma can get stuck in a place and leave behind residual feelings of unease, as well as unhappy spirits.

The old asylum is considered one of the most haunted locations in Michigan. Some visitors have reported seeing ghosts, including full-body apparitions. Many have reported feeling strange unseen forces or experiencing drastic changes in air temperature and energy. Bodiless voices and unexplained lights are often reported along with the sound of footsteps that echo in empty spaces. Construction workers have seen figures on the grounds; some of the workers became so terrified by what they saw that they refused to return to work.

There is an unsubstantiated story about a priest who allegedly hanged himself in the asylum's chapel. Some claim the priest was driven to suicide by dark spirits. There are also tales that religious objects cannot be taken into the building and that they mysteriously get destroyed before they can

Northern Michigan State Hospital.

be brought inside. Another unsubstantiated story involves a doctor who murdered patients and nurses.

Ghost hunters and reporters have captured unexplained voices on their tapes. Most often, the voices tell them to leave. Psychics have communicated with spirits who once lived on the grounds.

The laundry room is a hot spot of activity. Many have felt that they are being watched while there. Others have heard doors slamming, but there were no hands or wind to slam them shut.

Lights turn on and off by themselves. The scariest thing is that this even happened while the place sat empty—with no electricity.

The trails are a source of unease for some. Some feel like they are being watched as they walk the grounds, and others feel an extreme sense of unease. The tunnels are another creepy place where many spirits are seen. Some of the tunnels can be explored during the available tours.

One of the most popular stories involves the Hippie Tree, which is tucked deep in the woods behind the main campus of the old hospital. The remnants of this old willow tree have been painted bright colors, which has created a sprawling piece of creepy art. "The Hippie Tree is named such because of its place in local folklore. The tree is said to be a nexus for the unquiet spirits of those who once inhabited the hospital—and, by extension, the madness that haunted them. Visionaries, mystics, and other spiritual folks (hippies, as they were dubbed by the locals) would come to meditate beneath the tree and would then paint the products of their subsequent enlightenment on the warped limbs surrounding them," according to Atlas Obscura.

There are many rumors and legends about this haunted tree. Numerous otherworldly encounters have been reported by visitors. The tree supposedly houses a portal to hell that can be accessed if you approach the tree "just right." If you walk around the tree with the right combination of steps or movements, the portal will open. One urban legend details a 1950s murder. Two boys were playing in the woods by the old tree when an escaped inmate from the asylum found them. He murdered one of them and supposedly buried the body in a nearby spring. What happened to the other boy? Apparently, he got away to tell the story. Over the years, many of the tree's visitors have claimed that they have heard disembodied voices and had rocks thrown at them. Others just get a strange feeling that something is "off" in that location.

You can find the tree by parking in the lot at 1026 Red Drive in Traverse City. Go down to the trailhead, take the first right, proceed up a large hill, and go into a clearing. The next left will lead you down to the Hippie Tree. Look for the bright paint.

During the years the asylum sat empty, many haunting stories were born as curious explorers peeked in broken windows to see walls covered in peeling "institutional green" lead paint, deteriorating medical equipment, and empty halls filled with art made by patients and covered with graffiti from local vandals.

In 2000, the Asylum Preservation Board approached Ray Minervini. He was asked to help breathe new life into the old place. The board had a vision of transforming it into a "walkable, mixed-use village that would feature a wide variety of residential and commercial opportunities." The main focus was building 50, the large central building of the asylum. Many of the smaller outbuildings and cottages were torn down, while others were renovated or are still in stages of renovation. This project is so large it is still ongoing.

The location is now known as the Village at Grand Traverse Commons. It is filled with stores, cafés, restaurants, apartments, and condos. Events, festivals, and farmers' markets are held there. You can schedule a guided history or ghost tour. The grounds have many trails open to hiking, dog walking, and wandering.

One of the first restaurants to open at the newly renovated location was Trattoria Stella's. There are many reports of paranormal activity at the restaurant. When it first opened, it is said they had a hard time keeping staff because many were too spooked to work there.

There is no hotel on the grounds, but it is included in this book because there are apartments and condos available to rent through Airbnb. During the Halloween season, a few are advertised as "haunted" places to stay.

You can schedule a tour at www.thevillagetc.com/tour or find an Airbnb rental by clicking "Stay" along the top menu of the website.

CHAPTER 15

A HAVEN FOR THE PARANORMAL

THE COTTONWOOD INN, EMPIRE

9583 WEST FRONT STREET, EMPIRE, MI 49630

Nestled in the heart of Sleeping Bear Dunes National Lakeshore lies a charming old farmhouse surrounded by cottonwood trees and steeped in history and mystery—and perhaps containing a portal to the other side.

Known as the Cottonwood Inn, this quaint bed-and-breakfast, with its rambling porches and rustic red barn, beckons travelers seeking a unique experience along Lake Michigan's coast. A short stroll separates the inn from the shores of Empire Beach.

Andrew Roen was a Norwegian immigrant whose family came to the Empire area in 1892. He married Randi Holden. Roen, a pioneer in the now-defunct sawmill settlement of Norway Town, near Empire, initially worked as a lumber piler at the Empire lumberyard. Around 1900, he acquired and operated a saloon until Prohibition forced its closure. Roen's entrepreneurial spirit led him to purchase 133 acres of farmland, where he established his family home and fruit farm.

Andrew and his wife, Randi, raised five sons: Alfred, Andrew, Benhart, Gilbert, and Sievert. A sixth son, Reinhart Oliver Roen, born in April 1911, tragically passed away just sixteen days later.

Andrew Sr. passed away in 1946, and Randi passed away ten years later. The family matriarch's funeral was held in the home. Alfred and Gilbert pursued paths outside of the family farm, while Andrew, Ben, and Sievert remained on the land, never marrying or having children. Benhart was a teacher, but after his parents passed away, he ran the homestead. Andrew worked as a mechanic and loved to tinker with cars and motorcycles in his spare time. Ben and Sievert never saw eye to eye and would often argue. Sievert loved the orchards; that's where he would often escape to avoid Ben.

The brothers lived a quiet and frugal life on the farm. As they aged, they became increasingly reclusive, rarely venturing into town or mingling with others. Sievert would occasionally go into town and ramble on, telling everyone that his brothers wanted to kill him. It is thought that he was suffering from dementia. Because of the strange behavior, not too many people stopped in to visit the brothers.

In 1977, a mysterious twist unfolded when seventy-five-year-old Sievert vanished after a heated argument with his brothers. Despite extensive search efforts, Sievert was never found. Eight years later, he was declared legally dead. The mystery of Sievert's disappearance continues to haunt the town of Empire.

Fate took another cruel turn in 1985, when the two remaining Roen brothers, Ben and Andy, were discovered deceased in the farmhouse on a cold January morning. They had died within days of each other. Their bodies were found on January 17, 1985, by Gary Hilts and Dave Taghon, who had grown concerned after no one answered the phone for days. The medical examiner ruled their deaths natural, attributing Andy's passing to diabetic complications and Benhart's to natural causes.

Their deaths, however, catapulted the quiet men into local notoriety. Sievert's disappearance fueled speculation and rumors, with some suggesting foul play by his brothers. Others believed he wandered off and perished in the wilderness. A local psychic even claimed his remains lay hidden in the cistern, a notion disproven when it was inspected and found to be empty. These unanswered questions added to the farmhouse's growing mystique.

The reclusive brothers had no mourners at their funeral. Their cremated remains were interred quietly by a friend. Despite having wills, they remained unexecuted. A search for heirs revealed a nephew, Jack Roen, and his sister, Mrs. Fillingham, descendants of their brother Gilbert. They were joined by Alita Fisher, the daughter of their brother Alfred. Together, the three inherited the estate.

The Empire National Bank, appointed as temporary estate administrator, sealed the house for inventory, revealing a treasure-trove of family heirlooms. The house and outbuildings overflowed with antique furniture, trunks, and household items, preserved beneath layers of dust.

The Roens, averse to discarding anything, had meticulously preserved their possessions, including relics from their old saloon.

Among the discoveries was a substantial sum of cash. "We found more than $100,000 in cash in just the first hour of the first day," remarked Taghon to the *Leelanau Enterprise* in October 2000. "There was $20,000 in that bag we found in the filing cabinet," he added. "The rumors that money was stuffed all over the house weren't true. Most of it was in Social Security envelopes neatly stacked in a cabinet. Accounting for the money was written on the front of the envelopes. They kept careful records."

Their financial prudence extended to bank accounts and detailed financial records meticulously recorded in diaries. Every single cent was accounted for. Upon thorough assessment, the estate's value exceeded $450,000, a remarkable sum for three reclusive farmers.

The Roen brothers' deaths and the subsequent estate sale drew national attention, with over five thousand buyers from far and wide eager to acquire a piece of their mysterious legacy. Today, some of these items grace the Empire Area Museum, where the Roen Saloon has been re-created using the original back bar, main bar, tables, light fixtures, 1917 bar license, room partition, and tobacco cabinet.

The spirits of the Roen brothers may still reside at the farm. In addition to the Roen brothers' deaths, it is said that their grandmother Anna Holden passed away in 1925 on the farm, and a nurse (or possibly a lady friend of Ben's) also passed away in the home. After she was not seen for days, the doctor was called to check on her and found the ninety-two-year-old woman deceased in an upstairs bedroom. This was just a short time before Ben and Andy were both found dead.

Guests at the Cottonwood Inn have reported a wide range of paranormal experiences, from fleeting shadows and disembodied voices to full-body apparitions. Some have heard the eerie strains of a music box, despite no such instrument being found on the premises. The three rooms most notorious for paranormal activity are the Cottonwood, the Roen, and the Sunset Rooms. Andy passed away in the Roen Room. The nurse, Blanche, is said to have passed away in the Trillium Room.

The PXP paranormal investigation team, during their exploration of the inn, stumbled upon a chilling theory: the existence of a portal within the farmhouse that connects to the spirit realm. This portal, they believe, is frequently traversed by a malevolent little girl who seeks to lure unsuspecting guests into her realm. She also likes to crawl into bed with unsuspecting guests in the Roen Room.

One particularly unnerving incident occurred during a paranormal investigation led by Josh and psychic medium Tammy Schuster. A woman participating in the investigation was inexplicably scratched by unseen hands while in the Cottonwood Room. The scratch appeared instantaneously, leaving a visible mark on her leg. This unsettling encounter forced an abrupt end to the investigation.

Kathleen Tedsen and Beverlee Rydel also investigated the Cottonwood with psychic Tammy Schuster. They caught numerous EVPs that they believed belonged to Ben, Andy, and Sievert. They think they even caught snippets of the fight that led to Sievert's disappearance. They also came across an old freezer in the basement filled with something horrid and noxious. Photos of the contents showcased an image of what appeared to be a face—Sievert's face. The investigators strongly believe he was trying to reach out to them. He wants to be found; he wants the truth to be revealed.

The Cottonwood Inn's paranormal reputation continues to draw visitors seeking a glimpse into the unseen world. While skeptics dismiss the tales as mere folklore, the inn's rich history and the accounts from numerous witnesses point to the spirits of the Roen brothers and the strange little girl lingering at the inn, occasionally letting their presence be known to those who dare to check in.

PART IV
HISTORY AND SPIRITS IN EAST CENTRAL MICHIGAN

East Central Michigan is a region brimming with hidden gems, family-friendly adventures, and the allure of the local lakes. This area offers something for everyone—shopping, history, culture, art, and more. It includes Flint, Saginaw, Bay City, Lapeer, and portions of the Thumb Region.

The area is full of tourist attractions like Frankenmuth, Birch Run, the Flint Cultural Center, and Crossroads Village, all of which feature history and ghost stories waiting to be discovered. Flint and Bay City have numerous haunted locations detailed in the books *Haunted Flint* by Roxanne Rhoads and Joe Schipani and *Haunted Bay City, Michigan* by Nicole Beauchamp.

CHAPTER 16

WALTZ WITH RESTLESS SPIRITS AT THE WILLIAM PETER MANSION, COLUMBIAVILLE

4707 WATER STREET, COLUMBIAVILLE, MI 48421

Nestled in the heart of Columbiaville stands the William Peter Mansion, a majestic Italianate beauty shrouded in whispers of the past and chills of the paranormal. Its story begins with a self-made millionaire William Peter and his spirited wife, Roxana Clute.

William, a stowaway from Germany, arrived in New York and worked in the lumber industry. By the 1850s, he had become a millionaire with his hands in a little bit of everything, including lumber, banking, and farming. In 1852, he married Roxana Clute when she was just seventeen. Her father did not approve, so they eloped and settled in Toledo, Ohio, where their two children, Harriet and Alvin, were born.

Eventually, William Peter built more than just a fortune. He built a town, Columbiaville, laying its foundation in 1871. Gristmills, woolen mills, schools, churches, and houses for his workers—Peter's legacy extended beyond boardrooms and timber stacks.

But in 1892, it was time for a haven of his own. William Peter picked a site right in the middle of town on the corner of Second and Water Streets. The majority of the layout and design for the beautiful Italianate building was done by Roxana. Many of the materials used in the mansion's construction came from Peter's own companies. The wood was shipped from the Peter factories in Toledo and Bay City. The brick was from the Peter brickyard. Marble from Europe added a touch of elegance to sinks and tubs.

William Peter Mansion.

The Peter family moved into the sixteen-room mansion in 1896. Tragically, William's enjoyment was short-lived. He passed away in 1899, leaving Roxana to steward their grand estate until she passed away in 1917.

Time marched on, and the mansion witnessed a kaleidoscope of transformations. The Lapeer County Historical Society placed a historical marker on the lawn in 1972. The mansion was registered with the National Register of Historic Places in 1979. In the 1980s, the mansion was owned by the State of Michigan and turned into low-income housing. In the 1990s, it sat empty. Then, in 1998, fate intervened. Teresa Cook, drawn by a glimpse through an open door during a yard sale, found herself holding the keys to the mansion's future. With family by her side, she embarked on restoration, breathing new life into the crumbling grandeur.

For years, the William Peter Mansion was a haven for the curious. Ghost hunts, murder mystery dinners, and even witches' balls drew visitors eager to brush shoulders with the mansion's spectral residents. On National Ghost Hunting Day in 2018, the William Peter Mansion was one of 150 sites around the world to participate in the World's Largest Ghost Hunt. Two teams of paranormal experts led guests on a ghostly hunt in the house. HauntedJourneys.com described the William Peter Mansion as one of the most haunted places in Michigan.

With whispers of a dancing lady in the old ballroom, apparitions on the grand staircase, and unexplained noises throughout the building, the William Peter Mansion has earned its reputation as a paranormal playground. EVP recordings, phantom footsteps, and even levitating fruit add fuel to the fire, keeping the spirit world alive within these walls. The main staircase leading

Bed-and-breakfast sign.

to the second floor is a haunted hot spot. Many have seen the ghost of a woman dressed in Victorian clothing. Over the years, many guests have reported hearing whispers and seeing doors open and close on their own. Some people have heard footsteps when they knew no one else was in the building. EVPs have been recorded in the attic, sometimes accompanied by unexplained knocking. Groans and moans have also been captured on digital recordings. One investigator captured the voice of a little girl.

Investigators believe at least five spirits linger, one named Lucy. Their voices and movements echo through the halls. Even the apartment building on the grounds boasts ghostly tales, one involving levitating apples and unseen presences.

In late 2023, the William Peter Mansion embarked on a new chapter, welcoming new owners who plan to continue its legacy as a bed-and-breakfast and event center. As the doors reopen, so do the whispers of the past, beckoning curious souls to experience the magic and mystery that lie within the walls of this haunted haven.

So if you find yourself at the William Peter Mansion, listen closely for whispers from the resident ghosts forever bound to this haunted mansion.

CHAPTER 17

COLD SPOTS AND SPIRITED CONVERSATIONS

THE CADILLAC HOUSE, LEXINGTON

5502 MAIN STREET, LEXINGTON, MI 48450

The Cadillac House, nestled in the heart of Lexington, is more than just a charming historic inn. It is a vessel of time, telling tales of a bustling past and harboring restless spirits.

Built in 1859, the Cadillac House was a beacon of hospitality in Lexington's golden era. It served as a vital hub for travelers drawn to the region's thriving lumber and fishing industries. The grand opening was celebrated on Independence Day in 1860 with a parade and ball.

The hotel survived numerous fires in the 1870s that engulfed other buildings nearby; it even survived the Great Thumb Fire of 1881.

By the late nineteenth century, the *Detroit Free Press* described the Cadillac Hotel as "a charming retreat for the summer months." At the time, Lexington was becoming a popular resort town on the shore of Lake Huron. It was easily accessed by steamers and freighters on their way to and from Port Huron.

At the turn of the twentieth century, many of Lexington's major industries were closing. The local brewery, foundry, and organ factory all closed. The woolen mill burned in 1900, and a freshwater hurricane hit the area in 1913. Many ships and lives were lost during that deadly storm. After that, shipping centers and factories moved to Port Huron. That left the resort industry to provide for the town.

Throughout the Great Depression, Prohibition, and postwar, the resort industry kept the town stable. In 1940, the new owner, P.F. Rice, renamed the business the Rice-Cadillac Hotel.

In the 1950s, the resort era was in serious decline, and the Cadillac began to advertise itself just as a bar and restaurant. In the 1970s, the Cadillac was extensively remodeled and made to look like a Swiss chalet. In 2001, new owners took over and kept operating it as a bar and restaurant.

The Cadillac once again exchanged hands in 2016. The Roxbury Group invested over $3.5 million, removing all the 1970s renovations and restoring the building to its original 1860 glory while integrating modern conveniences and style. They also expanded, adding eleven guest rooms, and turned another building into a beautiful event space. They reopened in 2018 as the Cadillac House Inn and Tavern.

Over the years, whispers of ghostly encounters have permeated the halls of the Cadillac House. Guests have reported unexplained noises, fleeting shadows, and a sense of unease in certain areas.

One of the most commonly reported encounters involves "George." Guests have reported seeing his spectral figure seated at the bar, ordering a drink and engaging in conversation with other patrons, only to vanish when approached. Some say George was a guest at the inn and died during his stay; others say that he was murdered at the inn and can't leave until his killer is revealed. There is a bullet hole in a balcony door sealed with clear silicone so you can see right where the bullet went through. How it got there remains a mystery. Several paranormal investigators claim George isn't the only spirit who checked in but never checked out of this old hotel.

The Cadillac House Inn and Tavern offers guests a chance to mingle with the ghosts of the past while relaxing in comfort and style. So, if you find yourself in Lexington, consider spending a night at the Cadillac. You might end up sharing a drink with a ghost.

CHAPTER 18
LEFT BEHIND

THE HOLIDAY INN EXPRESS, FLINT

1150 ROBERT T. LONGWAY BOULEVARD, FLINT, MI 48503

Homes and buildings constructed on top of old cemeteries often have chilling tales connected to them. Often there are no facts to back up the rumors, but in Flint, the bones tell us a tale of being left behind when a cemetery was moved to a new location.

During renovations in 1985, a construction crew was horrified to discover the remains of more than two dozen people under the basement of the Holiday Inn Express (then a Hampton Inn) at 1150 Longway Boulevard and I-475. This chilling discovery forced the police and historians to do a little digging of their own—into the history of the location.

The hotel stood on the site of what was once an old cemetery. The Old Flint City Cemetery was created in 1842, while Flint was still a small village. The cemetery contained some of Flint's first settlers. By the 1950s, no one was taking care of it, and it had become overgrown. The City of Flint decided to redevelop the area. Starting in 1952, 1,199 residents of the Old Flint City Cemetery were removed from their graves and reburied at the New Flint City Cemetery on Linden Road and Pasadena Avenue. In 1958, the remaining residents of Old Flint City Cemetery, along with 122 grave markers, were moved to Avondale Cemetery's Pioneer's Row.

Or were they?

Local historians think that Albert J. Koerts, the man who purchased the Old Flint City Cemetery property, moved only headstones to Avondale, not

The Holiday Inn Express. *Photo by Joe Schipani.*

the remains. This means that the bones of Flint's early pioneers may still be under Flint buildings and parking lots, leaving their spirits to wander the city aimlessly. Koerts was killed in an automobile accident in 1969, taking the secrets of the Old Flint City Cemetery with him to his grave.

Now, restless spirits haunt the Holiday Inn, possibly hoping to reunite their bones with their gravestones. Many people have reported strange occurrences and ghostly visions at the Holiday Inn. One common phenomenon at the location is a loss of power with no known cause. Lights go out and electrical devices are suddenly drained of power. A former employee claims that doors would open and close by themselves and phone calls would come to the front desk from empty rooms. The calls were always dead air, with no voices or sounds to be heard. No one was ever found to be in the rooms making the calls. Many visitors have heard strange voices and seen shadowy figures. A male figure has often been spotted lurking among the shadows of the second floor. Several visitors have reported waking in the night to find a ghostly apparition standing at the end of their bed.

The bones found under the hotel were eventually reburied at the New Flint City Cemetery, but no one knows who they belonged to or which grave markers they should have been buried under.

Will a proper burial be enough to keep the ghosts who haunted the Holiday Inn happy?

Chapter 19

Where History Mingles with Modern-Day Spirits

The Linden Hotel, Linden

122 East Broad Street, Linden, MI 48451

Standing tall on Broad Street, the Linden Hotel isn't just a local landmark; it's a piece of Genesee County history, boasting the title of its oldest continuously operating business.

Its journey began in 1840, nestled at the corner of East Broad and Bridge Streets, back when the settlement was known as Warner Mills. In those early days, the hotel, then called the Exchange, was a beacon of hospitality, renowned for its delectable meals and comfortable lodgings. The arrival of the railroad in the late nineteenth century further cemented its popularity, attracting travelers and locals alike.

But as the twentieth century dawned and automobiles replaced carriages, the need for overnight stays dwindled. Enter Ed Dumanois, a visionary owner who transformed the Exchange into a fine dining destination. Motorists from Flint and beyond flocked to the hotel for elegant dinner parties and the chance to mingle with the elite. In 1921, Dumanois sold the Exchange to James and Emma Reip, who changed the name to House of Plenty. They catered to the elite, and their guest book featured well-known names in Michigan society. Private dining rooms were filled with governors, senators, and automobile company presidents all drawn to the House of Plenty's charm and prestige.

In 1954, after over 120 years on the corner, the hotel embarked on a new chapter, relocating to its current location on Broad Street. Jack Furry took the reins in 1993, continuing the tradition of hospitality with both lodging and dining until 1998. Sadly, in January 2021, Jack Furry passed away, but his two daughters continued to operate the Linden Hotel. Today, the upper floor houses the Crow's Nest, a lively sports bar catering to a younger crowd, while the ground floor retains the timeless charm of the Linden Hotel.

However, the hotel's story took a turn toward the paranormal in 1998. During a Civil War reenactment, a photo captured a chilling anomaly—a faceless Confederate soldier, sword in hand, standing among Union troops. No one present could identify the figure, and no one dressed in Confederate garb was present. This unsettling event was just the beginning.

Whispers of the unseen began to swirl. Keys jingled on their own, saltshakers took a tumble, and employees felt unseen hands tugging at their shirts. Empty rooms played host to shifting shadows, and a mischievous spirit seemed to have taken a liking to turning on the TV.

Paranormal investigators flocked to the Linden, drawn by its undeniable energy. Numerous paranormal groups have done investigations. Brenda Mikulka of South East Michigan Ghost Hunters Society captured an incredible photo of a ghostly young woman with blond hair dressed in a white nightgown standing on her tiptoes. The DJ booth in the Crow's Nest became a hot spot for strange occurrences, leaving even the most seasoned investigators feeling uneasy. Former owner Jack Furry believed the DJ booth was haunted by a man named Chuck, a longtime resident who never truly left. It's not known if he died at the hotel. A psychic confirmed this, revealing Chuck's fondness for the hotel and his reluctance to cross over. Other spirits, too, seem to linger within the walls. A young woman, rumored to have perished in a fire during a secret affair in the 1800s, has been sensed by several investigators.

David Tucker of Greater Michigan Paranormal Investigations left the hotel with an interesting video. Many other investigators have found "proof" of hauntings. It seems that several spirits lurk in the hotel in addition to Chuck and the ghostly young woman.

The Linden Hotel's walls continue to whisper tales of bygone eras, while shadows dance with the spirits of those who refuse to fade away.

CHAPTER 20

SPIRITS ABOUND AT THE FENTON HOTEL TAVERN AND GRILLE, FENTON

302 NORTH LEROY STREET, FENTON, MI 48430

Centered in the heart of Fenton, the Fenton Hotel Tavern and Grille boasts a history as rich as its aged spirits. But beyond its nineteenth-century charm and delectable tavern fare, something else lingers within its walls—whispers of restless spirits who refuse to check out.

The hotel was built in 1856, soon after the railroad made its way to Fentonville in 1855. Gazetteer, Seed, and Flint were the builders and owners of what they named the Vermont House. In 1868, Abner Roberts became proprietor of the newly named Fenton House. It became the DeNio in 1882, when D.W. DeNio purchased the hotel and gave it a facelift, complete with new wallpaper and furnishings. The Carpediem Club organized a fancy grand opening event with over two hundred guests. It was a roaring success. The DeNio House was one of the first Fentonville locations to get a telephone. DeNio continued to improve the accommodations. By 1886, it had a barn that could house one hundred horses and a hall thirty by eighty feet for public events. Mr. Hurd became the new proprietor in 1898 and restored the Fenton House name.

In 1916, T.J. Dumanois, owner of the nearby Linden Hotel, purchased the hotel. Soon after his purchase, Prohibition shut it down. After the repeal of Prohibition in 1933, the hotel reopened under the management of Arthur and Margaret Dumanois, T.J.'s son and wife. It is said that the Fenton Hotel was the first business to receive a liquor license in Genesee County after Prohibition.

The Fenton Hotel.

Over the years, the hotel continued to change hands, and the focus shifted to being a restaurant and event center instead of a hotel. The location received a state historical marker in 1971. In 1997, Nick and Peggy Sorise bought the building and renamed it the Fenton Hotel, opening it as a fine dining establishment. In 2006, the Sorises celebrated the building's 150th anniversary with renovations and an updated name: the Fenton Hotel Tavern and Grille. From the roaring success of the DeNio House to the quiet elegance of the Fenton Hotel, it adapted to the times, a hub for social gatherings and weary travelers.

Today, the brick building still stands at the corner of North Leroy and Main, looking much the same as it did in the nineteenth century. The only real difference is the front porch was torn off in 1904 by a team of runaway horses.

The Fenton Hotel is renowned as one of the most haunted bars in Michigan, its halls echoing with the whispers of the past. In 2019, Thrillest. com rounded up seventeen of the most haunted bars and restaurants in the United States, and the Fenton Hotel made the list.

The hotel has managed to keep a tight grip on its past. The dining room still features its original tin ceilings, and the foyer probably looks similar to the way it appeared in the early days of the railroad. It's easy to envision ghostly guests appearing in their nineteenth-century finery.

The second floor features a tiled ballroom, restrooms, and a room that once belonged to longtime custodian Emery. He worked there when the business was still renting rooms. The building stopped being a hotel in

1965. Even after Emery's earthly departure, he continues to maintain his post, albeit in a slightly more ethereal manner. Tools mysteriously shift, a popcorn maker turns on by itself late at night, lights flicker on and off, and the vacuum cleaner constantly gets unplugged—all attributed to Emery's diligent, if slightly mischievous, spirit. But the scariest thing is the footsteps many employees hear from upstairs after closing time. Heavy footsteps reverberating off the tin ceiling and thumps on the walls are nighttime occurrences that get blamed on Emery.

Emery's not alone. There are numerous spirits, like the phantom hugger who has been seen embracing staff when they felt no one. One employee would often hear someone calling her name even though she was alone. Then there's the naughty, flirtatious ghost who gets a little too familiar with female waitresses. There's also a mischievous entity that delights in shattering wine glasses.

The bar and dining room hum with paranormal activity, especially during December, when the festive spirit seems to amplify the ghostly encounters.

The third floor, once home to the hotel's more budget-conscious clientele, harbors its most chilling secrets. Whispers of a working girl who met her tragic end in the restroom's third stall linger, and women report strange chills and unseen brushes in that very spot.

Full-fledged apparitions grace the Fenton Hotel's halls. A black cat flits through shadows, a bearded man peers from a second-story window, and a tall figure in a top hat adds a touch of Victorian elegance to the proceedings.

The most popular spirit is undoubtedly the man at table 32. A Jack Daniels devotee, he continues to haunt his favorite seat, ordering drinks and then vanishing before the waitstaff can deliver them. Sometimes he is alone; other times he piggybacks off the drink orders of other people seated at the table, only for the waitstaff to return with drinks and discover no man at the table ordered a Jack and Coke. He has been seen by staff and patrons numerous times.

The Fenton Hotel's spectral residents aren't confined to its walls. One reporter visited the hotel with her husband, investigating it for a Halloween article. They became haunted. The entity, initially mocking their investigation, followed them home, bringing with it a trail of unsettling phenomena. Shadow figures, doppelgangers, whispers in the night, and unexplained scratches became their new reality, forcing them to seek professional paranormal help.

The Fenton Hotel's spirits have been referred to as guests who can check out but never leave, yet something left and followed this woman home.

CHAPTER 21

RENOVATIONS STIR UP GHOSTS AT THE WHITE HORSE INN, METAMORA

1 EAST HIGH STREET, METAMORA, MI 48455

Lorenzo Hoard and his wife, Lucy Carpenter Hoard, moved from New York to Metamora in 1850 and purchased a general store. They remodeled it and named it Hoard House, an inn and stagecoach stop. Rumors say it also became a stop on the Underground Railroad, and it was included in the book *Hauntings of the Underground Railroad: Ghosts of the Midwest*.

When the Michigan Central Railroad came through Metamora in 1872, the inn became a popular place for train passengers to stay for fifty cents a night. In the 1876 *Atlas of Lapeer County*, Hoard House was noted for having "good accommodations for travelers, feed and stabling for horses."

In 1905, William Deter and August Miller of the Deter House purchased Hoard House. During the Prohibition era, owner Frank Peters changed the name to the White Horse. Over the years, the White Horse passed through numerous hands. It has been a dance hall, boardinghouse, bar, ice cream parlor, and restaurant.

Drawn to its history and its future possibilities, Tim and Lisa Wilkins purchased the White Horse in 2001. In 2012, they made the difficult decision to close because it needed too many costly renovations. At the time, it held the state title for the longest continuously operating restaurant.

Victor Dzenowagis and his wife, Linda Egeland, purchased the restaurant, knowing the village of Metamora needed the White Horse. They did

Left: Hoard House historical plaque.

Right: The White Horse sign.

extensive renovations and reopened in 2014. Over $3 million went into reviving the White Horse. The result is exquisite.

Craftsmen, architects, stonemasons, farmers, businesses, and an artist from France all contributed their skills and resources to help create something unique and beautiful. The dining room floor was created by Metamora resident John Yarema with wood from thirty-five cherry, red maple, and white oak trees taken from the grounds of Dzenowagis and Egeland's eighty-acre farm in Metamora. The wood was milled by a fifth-generation sawyer in Lapeer. The main dining room chandeliers are antique hay hooks from a nearby 1880s barn. Stones from the same barn are now the inn's massive fireplace and chimney, which were constructed by members of the local Giddings family, who have been stonemasons for at least three generations. The fireplace mantel is a beam from the same barn. French artist Jean Louis Sauvat added the large charcoal horses on the wall of the main dining room.

The couple restored the original structure that belonged to Lorenzo Hoard but tore down many of the additions that had been added over the years. They added a large side patio overlooking a staging area for carriage and sleigh rides, an elevator, new upstairs bathrooms, a balcony, and a much larger kitchen.

Lorenzo Hoard died in 1888, but it seems he never left. Many think Lorenzo has stayed on to be the caretaker and protector of the old inn.

Owner Linda Egeland, a former chemist who never believed in the supernatural, thinks Lorenzo is still around. She even said in a 2014 *Detroit*

Free Press interview that "our manager, Chris, was in the basement and took a picture there…with a ghost standing in it. It looks like a guy in suspenders. It looks like a farmer."

The old building has many unexplained cold spots, creepy creaking stairs, slamming doors, ghostly footsteps, and flickering lights—all with no human source. Staff members often feel like they are being watched even when no one is around. A current staff member at the White Horse is terrified to close at night. The building is so spooky that he never wants to be alone in the place.

A legend claims that several men and a barmaid were killed in a fire in the front section of the bar. Guests have sworn they heard screams and moaning in that area—could it be from those who perished in the fire?

South East Michigan Ghost Hunters investigated the White Horse, and one of their team reported seeing a young male watching the inn's staff. They caught quite a bit of activity, including some orbs on film. Paranormal investigators are divided on orbs. Some swear they are nothing more than dust and light, while others are adamant that orbs are otherworldly energy. This author visited the White Horse for a delightful dinner, and there wasn't an orb in sight. The only spooky thing I experienced was a couple of unexplained cold spots in the hallway and restroom.

Over the years, many apparitions have been seen on the premises, including escaped slaves, a man dressed in a 1940s-style tuxedo, a young girl, and an old man.

CHAPTER 22

HAUNTING HOSPITALITY

THE HOLLY HOTEL, HOLLY

110 BATTLE ALLEY, HOLLY, MI 48442

Ghostly giggling and the spirited playing of a piano are just two of the hauntings at the famous Holly Hotel, which is often advertised as Michigan's most haunted building. In 1989, world-renowned parapsychologist Norman Gauthier concluded that the building was "loaded with spirits." In 2009, it was included in the Travel Channel's show *The Most Terrifying Places in America*.

In the 1880s, Holly was a bustling railway town. The location of the hotel began as a modest two-story wood building that stood on the property where the Holly Hotel now resides. The Hirst Hotel was built in 1891 by John Hirst as a railway inn. Over twenty-five trains passed through Holly daily. The busy railway town was full of activity. Saloons lined Martha Street, and so many brawls broke out that it soon became known as Battle Alley. The name stuck, and the street is still known as that today.

During the early 1900s, the hotel was the hub of social activity in Holly. Many groups and organizations used the space for meetings, and Sunday dinner was an elegant affair.

On August 29, 1908, Carry Nation made her infamous visit to the Holly Hotel. Nation and her pro-temperance supporters stormed the town, wreaking havoc by clubbing patrons of the hotel with their umbrellas. A painting of a scantily clad lady above the hotel bar enraged Carry further, and she proceeded to smash all the whiskey bottles with her trademark axe. She was appalled by John Hirst's attitude when he refused to condemn the locals' drinking habits. Hirst had her arrested, and she was lodged in

Holly Hotel. *Wiki Commons, image by Andrew Jameson CC License.*

the local jail. Governor Warner used Carry Nation's incarceration as a political reason to visit Holly.

For many years, Holly held a Carry Nation Festival, and the hotel would offer special menus, a reenactment of her visit, and reduced prices on drinks. The festival was later changed to Holly Days.

The red brick Queen Anne building still stands at the corner of Broad Street and Battle Alley after surviving three fires, the first two exactly sixty-five years apart. On January 19, 1913, the hotel burned for the first time. Exactly sixty-five years later to the date and the hour, the Holly Hotel burned again on January 19, 1978. After the second fire, it was remodeled and no longer featured guest rooms but focused on dining and entertainment.

The third devastating fire happened on the summer solstice, June 21, 2022. The six-alarm fire devastated Holly. The hotel and two other buildings burned, including the beloved store Battle Alley Arcade Antiques, which was reduced to rubble. Firefighters worked for hours trying to put out the blaze.

Many took to social media to share memories of their time spent at the hotel. For decades before the pandemic, the hotel hosted a comedy club.

Tim Allen, Bill Maher, Judy Tenuta and Soupy Sales were just a few of the big names who graced the club's stage. The comedy club had just been renovated into a jazz and blues club the October before the fire.

During the Halloween season every year, the hotel would offer witch-themed tea parties and evening séances. The séances were a great time to meet the resident spirits and ghosts who just came to say hello to séance guests.

Ghostly encounters happen most often on the stairs and in the Carry Nation Banquet Room.

Mr. Hirst, the original owner, makes his displeasure known every time renovations occur. If you spot a man wearing a frock coat and top hat, you've probably encountered Hirst. If the aroma of cigar smoke accompanies him, it's definitely Hirst. Cigar smoke is a telltale sign Hirst's spirit is roaming about. Occasionally, the faint sounds of his baritone laughter will drift throughout the hotel.

The haunting sound of a woman singing far away can sometimes be heard echoing through the hallways. The spirit of former hostess Nora Kane loves to play piano and sing for guests. The scent of her perfume still wafts through the former hotel, the floral aroma often manifesting in the turret area of the main bar. Kane's image has appeared in photos taken in the hotel, most often in wedding photos. Her spectral image has also appeared in an ornate mirror.

Two ghostly girls hang out in the kitchen giggling and playing with utensils. One is thought to have been killed during a nearby stable accident. One of the girls' favorite toys is a meat cleaver. Some think one of the girls was Nora Kane's daughter. The ghostly girl is described as being between nine and thirteen years old with red hair.

Other resident spirits include the Hirsts' dog, Leona. Her phantom barking has been heard by employees, and they feel the canine's spirit rubbing on their legs early in the mornings.

A Native American spirit has also been seen. In February 1996, Mrs. Kutlenios had arrived to set up Thursday afternoon tea when she encountered him. He looked real as can be, except he had no feet. He just hovered in the room for a moment before disappearing. Spooky shadows have been seen twisting and turning through rooms during séances before abruptly disappearing right into the wall. Numerous investigations have been done. Everyone seems to agree this hotel is haunted.

At the time of this writing, the hotel is still rebuilding after the last devastating fire. The owners hope to reopen as soon as possible.

STEP BACK IN TIME
AT CROSSROADS VILLAGE, FLINT

6140 NORTH BRAY ROAD, FLINT, MI 48505

Crossroads Village is a location where the past and the present collide. Modern-day tourists roam the village, enjoying a glimpse of the past and seeing how people lived in the late 1800s while never having to give up their modern conveniences like cellphones or Wi-Fi. The village is a liminal space, stuck in the past while simultaneously existing in the present.

With buildings and train cars so old, it's hard to imagine there isn't a ghost or two attached to them, but have no fear—the stories whispered of ghosts of Crossroads aren't scary. It seems several residents just continue to linger in the places where they lived and died. Some like to play pranks, while others are just shadows of the past, time slips showcasing an era gone by. Echoes of happiness and laughter linger, mixing and mingling with the village visitors.

Numerous former employees at Crossroads have experienced the feeling of eyes watching them wherever they go in the village. One said, "You're never alone, even when the buildings are empty."

Crossroads Village opened on July 4, 1976, but the preservation of several of the structures started in 1967, when the historic buildings were going to be demolished to make way for the I-475 freeway. Ken Smithee moved them to their current location. At that time, there was no plan other than to keep them safe.

In December 1968, a proposal to save the old buildings and reassemble them as a museum was presented to the Genesee County Board of

Commissioners by John West and Stanley Mahaffy. The Genesee County Parks and Recreation Commission, Genesee County Historical Society, Flint Beautification Commission, Flint Housing Commission, the Mallory Charitable Trust, the C.S. Mott Foundation, and many others were engaged in the project.

In June 1969, the Buzzell House and Judge Wisner's carriage house were the first to be rescued; they were soon followed by the Eldridge House (1860s). The Genesee County Parks and Recreation Commission granted $20,000 to move the first two buildings to land donated by the C.S. Mott Foundation.

During the summer of 1973, the Genesee County Board of Supervisors provided funding to begin their bicentennial project; the plan was approved in 1974, and more historical buildings started being moved to the property. This continued throughout the 1970s and '80s.

In 1981, the Attica Hotel (1870s) was moved from Lake Pleasant Road in Lapeer County to the Village. The Attica architecture is a mixture of Greek Revival and Colonial.

It was built by lumber baron William Williams, but sources have conflicting dates about the build year—some say 1850 to 1858, while others note it was built in the 1870s. William and Betsey Williams lived in the house with their

The Attica Hotel in Crossroads Village.

fourteen children. Around 1881, the building became the Schirmer House. Over the years, it was a post office, an apartment building, multiple stores, and, of course, an elegant hotel with a second-floor ballroom that opened onto the balcony.

Attica residents loved to regale each other with tales of ballroom brawls and people going over the balcony. The hotel survived a fire in the early 1900s.

A ghostly woman in white is often spotted on the balcony of the Attica Hotel.

The building is now a store inside Crossroads Village.

A PIECE OF THE PAST: MASON TAVERN INN

6140 North Bray Road, Flint, MI 48505

Daniel Mason was a native of New Hartford, New York, before immigrating to Michigan. He built the structure in 1850 as an inn and tavern sitting at the corner of Fenton Road near the crossing of Grand Blanc Road.

It became a popular stagecoach stop along the route of the Flint and Fentonville Plank Road Company. From 1853 to 1871, Mundy Township's

Opposite: The Mason Tavern Inn.

Above: The Mason Tavern Inn at Christmas.

first post office was also housed inside the Mason Tavern. The tavern and post office continued to operate until the Flint and Pere Marquette Railway came to the area, which routed people away from the stagecoach stop. In 1879, Mason sold the property and moved to Flint, where he died in 1880.

It was a private residence until Crossroads Village relocated the Mason Tavern Inn to this property. It was cut into three pieces so it could be moved.

The inn reopened to the public in 2010. A worker passing out candy during the Crossroads Ghosts and Goodies event that year continually felt someone tugging at her hair and her cloak, though no one was ever there. Someone from beyond really wanted her attention.

CHAPTER 24
LOST IN LIMBO

SWEET DREAMS INN, BAY PORT (FORMER INN)

The Bay Port area was first settled in the 1860s when 140 German immigrants created a religious commune in the wilderness called Ora Labora. The colony was plagued by illness and within months had lost one of the little girls. The Old Bay Port cemetery was established in 1863 on the extreme southern edge of the Ora Labora colony. This remnant of the long-lost colony is all that remains of Ora Labora.

William H. Wallace was a prominent Bay Port citizen who owned Wallace Stone Quarry. Wallace dabbled in politics and was a delegate in the Republican National Convention in 1908, 1916, and 1924. He was president of Michigan Sugar Company and Bay Port State Bank. In 1895, Wallace and W.J. Orr established the Bay Port Fish Company.

Wallace built a Victorian mansion in 1890 for his family. They lived on the first and second floors. The third floor was a large ballroom with vaulted ceilings. Local historians said that every Saturday, Wallace hosted parties filled with music and dancing that lasted long into the night.

William Wallace's first wife, Elizabeth, passed away in the home in 1893 surrounded by her husband and children. Supernatural Seekers paranormal investigators discovered they also had two children who passed away in the home. William was killed in an automobile accident in 1933.

The Wallace home remained in the family for over one hundred years until Betty Rapson bought it in the 1980s and turned it into a bed-and-breakfast. Renovations revealed secret passageways that connected all the rooms on the second floor. Were they for the maids? Or for bootleggers during Prohibition? No one knows. The space of the passageways was used to add bathrooms to all the bedrooms.

In July 2001, Julie Chaperon purchased the B&B and changed the name to the Sweet Dreams Inn. She never intended for it to be a "haunted hotel" experience, but that's what it turned out to be. She had to set up a strict no-refund policy because throughout the years, many guests left early due to ghostly disturbances, specifically those who stayed in the Peacock Room. Guests would wake Julie up in the middle of the night terrified, pounding on her door because whatever was in the room scared them so badly.

In the fall of 2003, two of Julie's friends stayed in the Peacock only to be awakened by what sounded like a loud party on the third floor. There was ballroom music and laughter; it even sounded like furniture was being moved around on a wooden floor. They went upstairs to see what was going on, but as soon as they reached the third floor, everything got quiet. Everyone was sleeping in the large carpeted suite. They returned to their room, climbed into bed, and the party started again, and it didn't stop until the sun came up. It seems Wallace's parties never ended.

The second floor has also been known to have activity. Julie and some of her friends had quite a girls' night in the winter of 2004. One of their friends retired early for the evening. Right after she left the group, things got crazy on the second floor. There was so much noise and laughter, and it sounded like children were running up and down the hallways. After a while, they checked on their friend, only to find her sound asleep in her room downstairs. She had never gone to the second floor. The group became scared, and several wanted to leave even though it was 2:00 a.m. Julie screamed at the ghosts to "Stop it!" and things finally got quiet and her friends stayed.

Julie embraced the inn's spirits and opened the doors to paranormal investigations and haunting events. The inn became one of the most popular haunted locations to visit in the state because of the amount of paranormal activity people would experience. The haunted inn was featured in several paranormal books, a documentary, and a movie. Quite a few Michigan newspapers and local TV channels featured reports of spooky activity at the inn.

Many visitors said they heard someone whispering in their ear even though no one was near them. William Wallace's heavy boot steps still echo in the halls, and the sounds of children running and playing are often heard. The spirit of Mrs. Wallace has often been seen on the second floor going in and out of rooms and checking on her five children, and a young spirit haunts the third floor and is often seen gazing out of windows.

Another spirit is believed to be Ora Wallace, the daughter of William and his second wife, Frances. The story goes that Ora was quite the wild child and would climb out of her bedroom window to go into town so she could go drinking and carousing with boys. Eventually, her mother locked her in a room so she couldn't escape.

Many ghostly things have happened at the inn—beds moving, mattresses being pushed up from below, and doors opening and closing on their own.

A nearby stagecoach stop brought travelers to the Bay Port Hotel that once stood along the waterfront across the street from Wallace's home. In the late 1800s, Bay Port was quite the tourist destination, and the Bay Port Hotel was one of the finest in Michigan—a three-story structure with a stone foundation set on solid rock. The website Thumbwind referred to it as a "modern hotel, with finely furnished rooms and broad verandas, surrounded by handsome shade trees, a bowling alley, and a billiard hall, [that] provide entertainment and amusement for the guests."

In 1900, a heartbroken young man committed suicide at the hotel and left bloody handprints all over his beautiful room. That seemed to be the beginning of the end for the luxurious hotel, as rumors swirled and stories were shared that the place was haunted. Guests claimed to have seen the ghosts of the young man and his betrothed, who preceded him in death.

Wallace purchased the failing hotel and tore it down in 1907. All that remains is a set of stairs overlooking the water, prime real estate that was never built on again. All that remains of the stagecoach stop is a historical marker and a large rock.

If you sit outside these haunting locations on a dark, quiet night, you may hear music and laughter from the third-floor ballroom of the old Wallace mansion or catch a ghostly glimpse of the old stagecoach pulling up like a pair of Sweet Dreams guests did in the autumn of 2005. As they sat outside enjoying a smoke, the sound of horses broke through the quiet night air. They turned toward the sound, and the sight of a shadowy stagecoach came into view for just a moment before disappearing into the darkness.

The inn is currently closed. At the time of this writing, it is either empty or has become a private home.

PART V
CULTURE, HISTORY, AND GHOSTS IN WEST CENTRAL MICHIGAN

West Central Michigan is filled with natural beauty, vibrant cities, and endless possibilities. This region offers culture, history, and numerous outdoor activities along Lake Michigan's shores and sand dunes. The area includes Grand Haven, Grand Rapids, Muskegon, Holland, and Saugatuck. West Michigan is considered to be extremely haunted. The Felt Mansion, the Holland Castle, and the Nunica Cemetery are some of the most spooky spots, while the downtown area of Grand Rapids is filled with haunted locations.

CHAPTER 25

A HAUNTING HISTORY

THE KIRBY HOUSE, GRAND HAVEN

2 WASHINGTON AVENUE, GRAND HAVEN, MI 49417

The Kirby House is considered West Michigan's most haunted location. It sits on the property that once housed Grand Haven's first permanent home, built by town founder William Ferry, who coincidentally happens to be connected to a couple of other haunted Michigan locations. Ferry's home burned down in 1866, but he did not rebuild. He and his wife moved in with their son, Thomas White Ferry, who had a mansion in Grand Haven. Thomas was a politician and served in the United States House of Representatives and the United States Senate for Michigan.

A hotel was built in 1873 where the Ferrys' log cabin had stood. Over the years, ownership has changed hands many times. In 1900, it became the Gildner Hotel. In 1947, it became the Schuler Hotel. Win Schuler removed the third floor in 1965 and turned the building into a restaurant. Schuler's Bar Cheese was invented in this spot. The Gilmore family purchased the building in 1989 and named it the Kirby House, and it now consists of three restaurants, a nightclub, a tiki bar, a billiards hall, an open-air deck, and several event rooms.

Strange occurrences have given the old hotel an eerie reputation. Many former employees had weird things happen—nothing too terrifying, just odd things that make you wonder. Unexplained voices, lights flickering…

Several specters have been spotted at the Kirby, including a young girl nicknamed Emily, a bride, a Civil War soldier, and a woman in Victorian clothing.

The Gildner, Grand Haven.

Taylor Schippers has worked at the Kirby House for over a decade. According to WZZM13 on October 31, 2022, "Schippers says one story has stuck with her all these years. After a birthday party in one of the restaurant's event spaces, a stray balloon wandered through the restaurant at chest-level, the height it would be at if a child was holding it. She explains it was quite an eerie sight for her and her coworkers as they watched it work its way through the large dining room. Schippers believes the balloon incident could've been the ghost of Emily. A medium who visited the restaurant told Schippers a young bride was haunting the halls, who was apparently killed when she was pushed down the stairs."

Paranormal researcher and author Amberrose Hammond said that the ghost of Emily is often seen on the stairs in the main dining room. The woman in Victorian clothing is usually found in the basement wine cellar. EMF readings spike in one particular corner of the basement wine room, a spot where another apparition has been seen.

Reverend William Ferry, the man whose home burned down in 1866 on the land the Kirby House now sits on, is tied to another Grand Haven ghost story and has ties to Mission Point on Mackinac Island. Ferry was born in Granby, Massachusetts, in 1796. He was ordained by the New York Presbytery in 1822 after attending the New Brunswick Seminary. He was appointed as a Presbyterian missionary to the residents of Mackinac Island.

He married Amanda White, and they founded a missionary on the island in 1823. The Mission House was built in 1825. Five of their seven children were born on Mackinac Island. The family left the island after the fur trade began to dwindle. They arrived by boat at the mouth of the Grand River on November 2, 1834. Ferry is considered to be the founder of Grand Haven.

There is an urban legend surrounding Grand Haven's Lake Forest Cemetery. In the middle of the cemetery, you'll find an old winding stone staircase that ascends to the top of a hill. The "Stairway to Hell" is the site of numerous reports of paranormal activity. Legend has it that whenever someone new is buried in the cemetery, their soul is forced to climb that stairway to receive its judgment. If they are destined for heaven, a white light will appear at the top. If the soul reaches the peak of the hill without receiving a light, then they are damned and sent back down the hill, where hell awaits.

These proceedings are watched over by a glowing blue man who has been identified by many as none other than the Reverend William Ferry. The Ferry family plot is at the top of the hill. Some stories suggest Reverend Ferry simply watches over the cemetery, emitting an eerie blue glow as he sits among the tombstones. Paranormal investigators have found evidence of ghostly activity throughout the cemetery ranging from full-blown apparitions to glowing lights emanating from cracked gravestones.

Two of Ferry's sons served in the Civil War. Major Noah Ferry was killed in the Battle of Gettysburg. His body was retrieved, and he was buried in what became Lake Forest Cemetery. Lieutenant Colonel William Montague Ferry Jr. survived the war and later became mayor of Grand Rapids. He died in Park City, Utah, but his body was returned to Grand Haven to be buried. Could either of these men be the Civil War soldiers spotted at the Kirby? Did they return "home" after death?

Why is the Ferry family connected to multiple haunted locations?

PART VI
URBAN THRILLS AND GHOSTLY CHILLS IN SOUTHEAST MICHIGAN

Southeast Michigan is a multifaceted gem. Whether you crave urban thrills, peaceful escapes, or a taste of history, this region promises an unforgettable experience. The area includes Detroit and Lansing. Detroit has a wild history tangled with tales of the occult tied to more than one spooky spot, while the state's capital is filled with a variety of strange tales and haunted hot spots to explore, like the capitol building or the Stimson Hospital just outside Lansing in Eaton Rapids. For in-depth details about area haunts, read *Haunted Detroit* by Nicole Beauchamp and *Haunted Lansing* by Jenn Carpenter.

CHAPTER 26

HOTEL FORT SHELBY

FROM LUXURY HOTEL TO HAUNTED GEM, DETROIT

525 WEST LAFAYETTE BOULEVARD, DETROIT, MI 48226

In late 1917, Detroit witnessed the grand opening of the Fort Shelby Hotel, a beacon of modern luxury designed to cater to the latest trends. Inspired by E.M. Statler's groundbreaking hotel, Fort Shelby boasted innovations like a garage for automobiles, unheard of at the time.

John C. Thomson, Chas. A. Bray, and G. Brewster envisioned this masterpiece. They secured prime real estate at the corner of First Street and Lafayette Boulevard near steamer docks and Union Station, ensuring easy access to transportation, theaters, and shopping. Chicago architects designed a ten-story steel structure adorned with tapestry brick and cut stone. Amenities like modern heating, private baths, and Detroit's first servidor service—a compartment for room service requests—cemented the Fort Shelby's reputation as a leader in hospitality.

Success fueled expansion. A 450-room addition by renowned architect Albert Kahn in 1927 introduced the elite Empire Room, a cocktail lounge, and a dedicated conference floor. The Crystal Ballroom, complete with a stage and kitchen, became a hub for catered events.

However, the Great Depression dealt a crippling blow in 1930. By 1934, the owners were defaulting on their mortgage. Yet J.E. Frawley steered the hotel through turbulent waters, managing it through World War II's boom years. In 1951, Albert Pick Hotels Co. acquired the Fort Shelby, renaming it Pick–Fort Shelby Hotel. Frawley remained as vice president

Hotel Fort Shelby.

and director. Fortunately, Pick did not alter the hotel very much—just the dining areas—so the space retained its original architectural features.

The 1960s and '70s saw a decline in travel to Detroit. Union Station closed, and the Michigan Central Station was headed downhill. Railroads ceased to bring guests, and the Pick–Fort Shelby succumbed to its financial woes in 1973. Enter three enterprising twenty-something siblings—Jay, Neena, and Vivian Ross—who attempted a groovy 1970s-style transformation. Imagine a grand hotel mixed with the interesting style choices of the 1970s creating a wild party palace. It is no surprise that the hotel closed within three months. Some of the converted apartments kept residents and a few of the cafés and restaurants stayed open for awhile, but the 1917 portion of the building was sealed off. By the early '80s, pretty much everything was closed and left to ruin. One bar, Shelbys, clung to life until 1998. After that, the building sat vacant for almost a decade.

The year 2007 brought about a grand rebirth. A massive $90-plus million renovation resurrected the Fort Shelby as the Doubletree Guest Suites. Over two hundred guest suites and residential apartments rose from the ashes, preserving some of the original architectural marvels while replacing decaying elements. The Shelby reopened in December 2008 as the Doubletree Guest Suites Fort Shelby/Detroit Downtown.

Amid this revival, whispers of the past linger. Shadowy figures and apparitions reportedly roam the halls and guest rooms. One guest turned on the shower to steam their clothes and then forgot about the running water. Suddenly, they were startled by a dark figure dashing into the bathroom. Curiosity made them follow, and they discovered the tub was ready to overflow thanks to a plugged drain.

Urban legend claims that there was a homeless man named Al who was sleeping in the abandoned Fort Shelby's basement when a pipe burst and he drowned. Perhaps Al didn't want anyone else to drown and rushed in to remind the guest to turn off the water. Al is the most popular spirit in the hotel and is often spotted in the lobby, outside by the entrance, in the courtyard, and wandering the halls.

Another guest was staying in room 324, sleeping soundly, until the sound of someone entering their room woke them up. The door was still latched, and there were no signs of anyone being there. Perhaps the ghost just wanted to say hi.

Beyond the whispers of ghosts and legends, documented tragedies add layers of history. Suicides, sudden deaths, and even murder have left a dark stain under the glitz and glitter of the luxury hotel.

In addition to the rumors of Al's demise, several recorded deaths have occurred at the hotel over the years. In 1937, forty-six-year-old William Firth climbed into a bathtub full of water and shot himself. He checked into the hotel at 3:34 a.m. and was dead before 11:25 a.m. Thirty-eight-year-old Dr. Harry Shields checked into the hotel and downed several bottles of sleeping pills. A chambermaid found him unresponsive the next morning. A doctor was summoned, but Shields was unable to be revived. In 1933, an Alpena woman, Mrs. J.E. Richards, suddenly passed away in her Fort Shelby hotel room. Then in September 1951, May Laurie Moore, wife of the hotel's general manager Jerry Moore, passed away in her room at the hotel after a long illness.

The most shocking death at the Fort Shelby happened in 2010—and it was murder.

Twenty-three-year-old Diana Demayo had recently returned to her hometown after graduating from the University of Miami. She got involved with Peter Dabish, the wealthy but troubled son of the late Norman Dabish, a co-founder of Powerhouse Gym. On March 11, 2010, she was helping Peter move into his new place at the Fort Shelby apartments, which are connected to the Doubletree. A violently jealous Peter tormented Diana for hours in his apartment. It is said that he was drunk and in a jealous rage. He even called her father during the torment, saying she couldn't come to the phone because she was too busy crying. Peter stood six feet, five inches and weighed over 300 pounds. Diana was only five feet, one inch and weighed around 114 pounds. Autopsy reports show that she suffered at least eight blunt force blows to the head. After hours of torment, Peter eventually called the police and tried to say Diana overdosed on anxiety meds and hurt herself falling. But the apartment was covered in blood—so much blood. It was even in her dog's fur. Peter Dabish was convicted of torturing and murdering Diana Demayo. In November 2010, he was sentenced to life in prison with no chance of parole.

Despite the darkness, the Doubletree Fort Shelby and its apartments showcase the revitalized spirit of Detroit. Yet as guests traverse the hotel's opulent halls, they might just catch a glimpse, or a feeling, of the restless souls who once called the Fort Shelby home.

CHAPTER 27

ECHOES OF YELLOWSTONE AT THE TWO WAY INN, DETROIT

17897 MOUNT ELLIOTT STREET, DETROIT, MI 48212

Nestled in a Detroit industrial neighborhood, the Two Way Inn's ghostly tales and welcoming atmosphere draw visitors from far and wide.

The village of Norris was founded in 1873 by Civil War veteran and Yellowstone National Park superintendent Colonel Philetus Norris. Norris built the Two Way Inn, which originally served as the village's jail and general store. He lived there until his nearby home was built. The Two Way, known as Detroit's oldest bar, was turned into a saloon in 1876.

The Two Way Inn has survived over a century of Detroit transformation, from a stagecoach stop to a bustling saloon to a railway station, general store, hotel, jail, dance hall, and possibly a brothel. Rumor has it that a biker gang even called it home for a short period. Finally, it became the beloved neighborhood watering hole it is today. The Two Way Inn's walls echo with stories of those who have passed through its doors, from early settlers to factory workers, each leaving their mark on this historic establishment.

During Prohibition, it was owned by a dentist. Turns out the Volstead Act allowed doctors to prescribe patients up to a pint of whiskey every ten days. So a dentist could have alcohol on hand legally, making it a great cover for a speakeasy.

In May 2008, the *Metro Times* wrote, "The ghost's long white beard, cowboy hat, and buckskins seemed out of place when Henrietta Malak saw him one night three decades ago at the Two Way Inn, the north Detroit

Philetus Walter Norris.

watering hole she and her husband owned." For years, Malak wondered what an old frontiersman was doing in her industrial neighborhood. Years later, Malak's daughters were collecting historical information, and she saw a photo that helped her to identify the ghostly figure she had seen sitting on her bed. It was Colonel Norris.

Colonel Philetus Norris was quite a unique man—spy, poet, Civil War veteran, the list goes on. He was known as the man who put Yellowstone National Park on the map. He fought "to protect, preserve, and improve the Park." He was the second superintendent of Yellowstone but the first to receive a salary. Political maneuvering removed him from his Yellowstone position in 1882, and he moved on to the Smithsonian. Norris published a book in 1884 titled *The Calumet of the Coteau and Other Poetical Legends of the Border*, which included poetry and a guidebook to Yellowstone National Park.

Norris passed away in 1885 while in Kentucky collecting artifacts for the Smithsonian's bureau of ethnology. He recorded Native American culture. His son brought his body back to Michigan, and he was buried in Detroit's Woodmere Cemetery. But his spirit seems to prefer hanging out at the Two Way. He was a man of many talents and an American pioneer in his own right. He infused the bar with his adventurous spirit, forever etching his presence into its very foundation.

The Two Way Inn's paranormal reputation has only added to its allure. Over the years, countless patrons and staff have reported encounters with the bar's resident spirits. A shadowy figure is often spotted darting between the kitchen and restrooms.

Colonel Norris's spectral presence is the most prominent among the Two Way Inn's ghostly inhabitants. The colonel is said to roam the bar, his friendly demeanor welcoming guests to his historic establishment. The colonel's ghost is sometimes referred to as the Cowboy because of his wide-brimmed hat. At least two other spirits are roaming around the Two Way Inn, including a lady in white and a young boy. Several deaths have occurred on the premises, including one of the colonel's daughters and the dentist's son. Many say the lady in white is the colonel's daughter and the little ghost boy is the dentist's son.

The Two Way Inn's spirits are not malevolent entities but rather protective presences, watching over the bar and its patrons. Jennifer Isbister, granddaughter of the Malaks, has grown accustomed to their presence, referring to them as her "spirit friends." She believes their existence adds a unique charm to the bar, further enhancing its allure.

For those seeking a hauntingly unforgettable experience, the Two Way Inn beckons, but first you'll have to get buzzed in to the historic bar before you can immerse yourself in a space where the past and present mingle. Just don't ring the bell above the bar unless you are prepared to buy the entire bar a round of drinks.

CHAPTER 28

HAUNTINGS AND HISTORY AT THE MURPHY INN, ST. CLAIR

505 CLINTON AVENUE, ST. CLAIR, MI 48079

Long before Michigan became a state, the bustling St. Clair River town thrived with stagecoach travelers, riverboat crews, loggers, and fortune-seeking traders. Nestled along its banks, the Farmer's Hotel opened its doors in 1836, a beacon of hospitality in a rugged frontier. It boasted modern marvels for its time—an icehouse to keep food and drinks chilled and a stable for weary horses.

The first proprietor, Conrad Elpass, was a man shrouded in mystery. His brewing career preceded his foray into hospitality, but whispers of his darker side followed him. An 1891 liquor license violation and a 1902 assault charge cast shadows on his reputation. Yet the hotel thrived, witnessing the changing tides of time. The early twentieth century saw its transformation into the Scheaffer Inn, a name it bore for years before changing hands and monikers numerous times. Through it all, the inn's spirit remained.

Eventually, Larry and Dorothy Murphy took over, etching their name on the inn's history, naming it the Larry Murphy Inn. Today, the Murphy Inn holds the title of Michigan's oldest continuously operating inn, showcasing its enduring charm. The mid-1980s brought new owners, the Smiths and Sabotkas, who breathed fresh life into the aging structure with a new roof, updated plumbing, and electricity, along with a revamped interior. The Irish theme, however, remained, evident in the menu's corned beef and cabbage and playful Irish egg rolls.

Beyond the tangible history, whispers of another kind linger within the Murphy Inn's walls. At least three spirits call it home, forever bound to the place they once roamed.

Dorothy Murphy, the long-reigning owner, is the most visible presence. Often seen in her old room, the Devonshire (room 206), she has been spotted numerous times in the mid-evening sitting at the end of the bed. Occasionally she is seen wandering restlessly through the inn, especially in the late evenings. You might even catch a glimpse of her behind the bar or in the kitchen, embodying the inn's spirit of hospitality even in the afterlife.

Room 207, the Lancaster, harbors a different spirit—a shadowy gentleman. Two teenagers captured his chilling essence in a selfie. They discovered his ghostly figure looming in the bathroom after snapping the picture. This discovery sent them screaming from the room. This gentleman, affectionately dubbed "Rob," also frequents the bar and dining area, sending shivers down spines with phantom taps on shoulders and brushes against patrons who turn around to find no one there.

Whispers of a child's laughter echo in the basement, sending chills down owner Mitch Kuffa's spine as he searched for the unseen source. Paranormal investigators have confirmed the presence of this playful spirit. One researcher even caught the chilling glimpse of a smiling young boy peeking out at her from the crawlspace.

Today, the Murphy Inn beckons with seven charming rooms, including the Lancaster and Devonshire, each whispering tales of the past. Step into the Murphy Inn, raise a glass, and listen closely. You might just be lucky enough to catch a glimpse of the history that continues to linger within its walls.

CHAPTER 29
GHOSTS OF THE AUTO INDUSTRY

THE ENGLISH INN, EATON RAPIDS

677 SOUTH MICHIGAN ROAD, EATON RAPIDS, MI 48827

This breathtaking Eaton Rapids mansion was built in 1927 on fifteen lush acres. The ten-thousand-square-foot masterpiece once echoed with laughter from lavish soirées hosted by Irving J. Reuter, Oldsmobile president and GM executive. He and his wife, Janet, named their opulent haven Medovue.

Reuter's rise was meteoric. From engineer to Remy Electric Company official, he caught the eye of General Motors giants after the merger in 1918. By 1925, he held the reins of Oldsmobile. Medovue became a glittering emblem of his success. From 1928 to 1936, its halls resounded with the clinking of champagne glasses and the murmur of influential conversations among the American automotive and business giants gracing its threshold.

The Reuters' reign at Medovue was etched in the pages of who's who, but in 1934, Reuter abruptly retired. Medovue changed hands throughout the years, starting with the sale to Charles Holden in 1936 and then to the Roman Catholic Church in 1940. Throughout the years of church ownership, it housed Cupertino College's Franciscan Friars and the Youth Unlimited Foundation's exceptional children.

In 1962, C.J. and Millie Sumner rechristened it Storybook Acres, weaving it into their convalescent home, later dubbed Ivy Manor. Dusty Rhodes arrived in 1989, breathing new life into the estate as Dusty's English Inn, a historic gem reborn as an inn and event center. In 1991, it was added to the State Register of Historic Sites. Gary and Donna Nelson bought the inn in

Reuter House, Eaton Rapids. *Photo by Kennethaw88, wikimedia commons cc license.*

1996, and their son Erik Nelson took it over in 2011. The English Inn has thrived with the Nelson family at the helm.

Today, the English Inn includes a restaurant, an authentic English pub, overnight lodging, and an event center. Four rooms are available for small event rental for fifteen to fifty guests. The Medovue Hall banquet center is available for larger events; it can easily accommodate fifty to two hundred guests.

Beneath the polished veneer, whispers of the past linger. While the inn remains discreet concerning its paranormal residents, the *Spartan Post* detailed the hauntings in April 2008, bringing to life the stories of three spirits who echo through the halls: the ghost of a bearded man dubbed "the farmer," a disgruntled bride, and a lady in white.

The farmer, a spectral figure with a gray beard, frequents the first-floor bathroom, causing startled guests to wait in vain for an unseen occupant. The bride, heartbroken and sorrowful, haunts the Avon Room and sometimes plays a sorrowful tune on the first-floor piano with unseen hands. The lady in white, a fleeting presence, graces the kitchen with her spectral form, a once welcome sight to a former employee who enjoyed her visits.

Several former staff members have experienced the unexplainable. Tables mysteriously set themselves, glasses shatter in midair, and strange occurrences send shivers down the spines of overnight guests, leaving them tight-lipped and reluctant to share with employees. The spirits, their identities lost to time, still linger, adding a touch of the otherworldly to this historic haven.

While the English Inn may choose to keep its ghostly tales private, the echoes of Medovue's past, both opulent and spectral, remain. So if you dare to venture beyond the manicured lawns and polished facade, remember, you might not be alone at the English Inn. You may be sharing space with those who called it home before, their stories woven into the fabric of history waiting to be discovered. Whether you seek a taste of its opulent past, a comfortable stay, or a brush with the paranormal, Medovue awaits, ready to unveil its many stories, one haunting tale at a time.

Chapter 30

History in the Irish Hills

The Walker Taverns, Brooklyn

13200 M 50, Brooklyn, MI 49230

Sixty-five miles west of Detroit is the fabled Irish Hills region. The Indigenous tribes of the area consider it to be a mystical land. In the mid-century era of road trips, the Irish Hills was a popular destination filled with roadside attractions, but early settlers considered the area quite fearsome. They thought it was filled with ghosts and bandits. The Irish Hills area is now a popular location for ghost hunters.

The historic Walker Tavern was built in 1832 for Calvin Snell. It sits at the corner of what is now Cambridge Junction, the intersection of US-12 and M-50. Sylvester and Lucy Walker purchased the tavern from Snell in 1842. They had experience running a hotel in New York and quickly turned the Walker Tavern into a stagecoach stop, inn, and tavern—a popular refuge for weary travelers.

Rumor has it one guest checked in but never officially checked out. A gentleman by the name of Hipsley from Van West, Ohio, signed the guest book in the 1840s and then proceeded to have a wild evening of cards and booze before retiring to his room. When morning came, he was nowhere to be found, and all that remained was a large bloodstain on the floor. His horse turned up days later, but Hipsley was never seen again. One ghost hunter asked who was haunting the tavern, and the recorded EVP reply was, "Hipsley." Several spirited anomalies have been caught on film in the tavern.

In 1853, Sylvester Walker built the Brick Walker Tavern directly across from the original tavern. The new tavern had a ballroom and was the site

Brick Walker Tavern.

of many a party. A snowy New Year's Eve in 1863 sent partygoers home early—and sent one woman straight to her grave.

After Sylvester Walker died in 1865, Lucy Walker sold both properties to Francis Dewey. In 1922, Fredrick Hewitt bought the brick tavern and transformed it into an antique shop, museum, and restaurant. Hewitt was acquainted with Henry Ford, who happened to visit the Walker Tavern from time to time. So Hewitt named a room after him, which prompted him to name other rooms after celebrities of the time. There was a Daniel Webster Room and James Fenimore Cooper Room. Then Hewitt decided to capitalize on the story of the "wealthy cattleman" Hipsley who was mysteriously murdered. He created a murder room to draw tourists in. It was his most popular room.

The white-frame Walker Tavern became a Michigan Historic Site in February 1958 and was added to the National Register of Historic Places in January 1971. It is part of the Cambridge Junction Historic State Park, which is thirty-five miles west of Ann Arbor.

The Brick Walker Tavern was placed on the National Register of Historic Places in 2007. It is privately owned. For years, it operated as a popular hotel and venue for elegant rustic weddings, but at the time of this writing, it seems to be closed.

PART VII
SPIRITED ADVENTURES IN SOUTHWEST MICHIGAN

Southwest Michigan has something for everyone, whether you're seeking the perfect beach escape, a taste of local charm, or an adventurous getaway. The area includes South Haven and Kalamazoo. In South Haven, Captain James S. Donahue's spectral form is still keeping watch over the lighthouse, while Al Capone's mistress Flora is said to be forever wandering among the graves at Hawks Head/McDowell Cemetery. The Kalamazoo Civic Theater is haunted by a spirit who likes to play the piano and perform on stage whether it has an audience or not. For more haunting tales in this area, check out *Ghosts and Legends of Michigan's West Coast* by Amberrose Hammond.

CHAPTER 31

A Historical Haunting at the Henderson Castle Inn, Kalamazoo

100 Monroe Street, Kalamazoo, MI 49006

Henderson Castle sits on top of the steep West Main Hill overlooking downtown Kalamazoo and the Mountain Home Cemetery. The gorgeous Victorian constantly tops the lists of Michigan's most haunted locations. It has been a featured location in three horror movies and has been the destination of many ghost hunters and paranormal investigators. The castle will sometimes offer haunted history dinners and tours.

Frank Henderson was a businessman who owned the Henderson-Ames Company and made his fortune supplying uniforms to the army. The tycoon was also a Freemason who specialized in producing regalia for secret societies and organizations.

His dream home was built on a plot of land that had been inherited by Henderson's wife. To construct the Queen Anne Victorian, Henderson hired a team of engineers and architects, including C.A. Gombert of Milwaukee, to design a castle on the steep hill. Construction of the ten-thousand-square-foot castle started in 1890 and was completed in 1895. The three-story castle cost over $70,000—the equivalent of more than $2.4 million in today's money.

The castle website describes, "The castle's exterior was constructed of Lake Superior sandstone and brick, and the interior wood included mahogany, bird's eye maple, quartered oak, birch, and American sycamore. The castle was built with 25 rooms in all and exemplified the most expensive tastes of the time."

Henderson Castle.

The home was completed in 1895, but Henderson didn't get to enjoy the beauty for long; he died in 1899. Mrs. Henderson remained at the castle until 1908. The house remained in the Henderson family until 1919, when Bertrand Hopper, president and treasurer of Kalamazoo Stationery Company, purchased it. In 1945, William Stuifbergen purchased the castle, and it was converted into apartment units. In 1957, the house was purchased to become the Kalamazoo Art Center, but when the Institute of Arts remained downtown, the castle became the property of Kalamazoo College.

In 1975, Dr. Jess Walker was the owner. In 1981, the house was purchased by Frederick Royce. In 2005, the property was sold to Laura and Peter Livingstone-McNelis, who turned the castle into a bed-and-breakfast. In 2010, the castle was purchased by Robert Jackson, who then sold it to Francois Moyet in 2011. The castle is currently a quaint bed-and-breakfast, vineyard, day spa, and restaurant owned by Master Chef Moyet.

I discovered the property in 2014 and decided I wanted to stay there and see what all the fuss was about. So I booked a two-night stay. We stayed in the Italian Room in the main tower. Upon arrival, I was awed by the castle's beauty but filled with unease. Suddenly, I didn't feel very good. I was extremely uncomfortable.

Everything was gorgeous on the surface, but if you looked closely, you could see the underlying shabbiness. This is to be expected in a building over one hundred years old with a new owner in the process of upgrading, but the entire place just seemed off to me.

My husband and I explored the castle and the grounds, checking out all the locations open to the public. It is a very pretty place, but I just couldn't shake an eerie feeling. To add to the creep factor, there was a very odd piece of art hanging in our room that unnerved us a bit. We showed it to the lady at the front desk; she had never noticed the weirdness. When you look at the art, it just looks like swirls, but when I took a photo of it, a person's face appeared inside. The room was beautiful but much too bright. There were no curtains to close, just big open windows. And it didn't get any better after dark. The roof lights stayed on and continued to shine directly onto our bed after 10:00 p.m., when they were "supposed to shut off." All that light wasn't very restful.

At one point, my phone, which was sitting across the room from my husband and me, turned on, opened the camera, and took a photo all by

Henderson Park postcard.

Henderson Castle.

itself. That was extremely weird. Throughout the night, I kept hearing noises in the bathroom. That can easily be chalked up to old pipes, but it didn't help my uneasiness.

After not sleeping well the first night and just feeling weird all day, we decided to leave early and head home. Surprisingly, the inn refunded our money for the second night since we decided to leave.

The Henderson Castle is often listed in the top ten most haunted places in Michigan. Once you see it, you understand why. The mansion sits on top of a hill and overlooks a large cemetery that dates back to the mid-1800s. It is the final resting place for many of Kalamazoo's most prominent citizens.

Visitors and staff report spirit activity such as ghostly footsteps, disembodied voices, and doors that open and close by themselves. People have also seen full-body apparitions and been touched by unseen hands. Numerous guests have been woken in the middle of the night by disembodied voices. One guest was even told to go away.

According to Denise Gowen-Krueger of the Southern Michigan ParaNormals, the ghosts of Henderson Castle are Frank and Mary Henderson, the castle's original owners; Clare Burleigh, a Spanish-American War veteran who served with the Hendersons' son; an unidentified little girl; and the spirit of a dog. SMP has investigated the Kalamazoo property multiple times and captured numerous EVPs.

A popular legend features an unidentified young girl ghost, rumored to be the daughter of a former owner. The story says that one day the girl fell off scaffolding while drawing on a crossbeam in the dining area. Supposedly, the markings were revealed during renovations. No history has been found to prove this story.

CHAPTER 32

HAVEN TO HIDEAWAY

THE NATIONAL HOUSE INN, MARSHALL

102 SOUTH PARKVIEW, MARSHALL, MI 49068

Believed to be a stop on the Underground Railroad, the National House Inn is the oldest brick building in Calhoun County and the oldest operating bed-and-breakfast in Michigan.

Colonel Andrew Mann built the inn in 1835; it was first known as Mann's Hotel. It opened on New Year's Eve 1836 with a ball, the first held in Marshall. The building served as a circuit court and a county meeting place. P.T. Barnum loved to set up there when his circus came to town. The circus would stand on land just west of the inn. The building also served as the state headquarters for the Democratic Party.

It exchanged hands many times over the years before closing its doors in 1878. It was then converted into a factory, Windmills and Wagons. In 1902, it was converted into eight luxury apartments. Dean's Flats survived into the mid-twentieth century before falling into disrepair. In 1976, Norm and Kathryn Kinney decided to restore the old building to its original purpose as an inn. Thanks to many volunteers, it opened on Thanksgiving Day of the same year.

One of the most popular ghost sightings at the inn is the lady in red. She's a local legend, a "lady of the night" who worked the area when the place was really run-down. She died at the inn and is rumored to haunt the place. Numerous town residents and guests have seen this mysterious lady in red wandering the area around the hotel as well as seeing her inside the

National House Inn.

building. She likes to hide women's clothing and jewelry and give the men a good scare.

In 2011, an oil worker staying at the inn was awakened around 4:00 a.m. by a woman in red straddling him on the bed, her body weight holding him down as she stared into his eyes, her face only inches from his. After a few moments of staring, she just vanished into thin air. The employee packed his things and went to work to tell his boss. He refused to stay another night at the National Inn.

The Blue Room is haunted by two distinct scents: floral perfume and tobacco smoke. The scents seem to manifest from the wall on occasion. Perhaps they belong to a couple of spirits destined to be entwined in that hotel for all eternity.

Paranormal investigators have uncovered many details about the inn, including a death at the top of the back staircase and the spirit of someone who was murdered in the building. Legends say a man was shot and fell right out of the door, his body falling onto Michigan Avenue. Some have experienced the ghostly echo of a gunshot that resonates throughout the building followed by the sound of a slamming door.

A few guests have encountered the spirit of a little boy named Jason. Dressed in 1800s period clothing, the poor spirit has been there awhile. He's sad and lonely, so he might reach out to those who are sensitive to spirit interaction.

CHAPTER 33
GHOSTS AND GRUB

THE STAGECOACH INN, MARSHALL

201 WEST MICHIGAN AVENUE, MARSHALL, MI 49068

This building on Michigan Avenue sat along the Detroit to Chicago stagecoach line. It has been a little bit of everything over the years. In 1836, it was a shoe store; in 1840, a livery stable; in 1841, it housed a newspaper, then a store, then a Baptist church. In 1850, the second floor was converted into a hotel. By 1857, the main floor housed a saloon. It has had many names over the years. From 1879 until 1908, it was known as the Tontine Hotel. Tom Brooks leased the building in 1951 and named it the Stagecoach. Today, the Stagecoach is a popular pub that serves the "best burgers in Southwest Michigan."

It has quite a colorful history, though who knows how much of it is true and how much is urban legends. Stories circulate that Abraham Lincoln gave a speech from the balcony during his campaign trail and that Al Capone rented a suite for business when he visited the area. It was also reported to be a stop on the Underground Railroad. Rumors of hidden tunnels, secret rooms, and faux fireplace escape routes are the perfect accompaniments for tales of runaway slaves and illegal booze. Tunnels are also great places for ghosts to hide.

There seems to be plenty of ghostly activity at the Stagecoach Inn. Glasses rattle for no reason, phantom footsteps echo on empty floors and stairs, and the sound of rattling bottles with no source trails down hallways, as if someone were pushing a cart full of booze. A jukebox turns on by itself. Employees have reported getting their hair pulled when no one else was around. The oddest report is a video the owner caught on the security camera one night of a fog that just floated down the bar until it suddenly vanished.

Many think the ghost of Zenos Tillotson haunts the old inn. He was one of the first proprietors of the establishment.

CHAPTER 34

A HAUNTING HIDEAWAY

LAKESIDE INN, LAKESIDE

15251 LAKESHORE ROAD, LAKESIDE, MI 49116

Nestled on the shores of Lake Michigan, the Lakeside Inn beckons travelers with its promise of a timeless retreat. Stepping into its grand ballroom, adorned with a majestic stone fireplace, is like stepping back into the grandeur of the early twentieth century. The expansive porch, lined with inviting rocking chairs, whispers tales of leisurely afternoons spent basking in the gentle breeze drifting off the lake. And just across the road, a private beach awaits, inviting guests to dip their toes into Lake Michigan's cool water.

The Lakeside Inn is filled with a rich history. Designated as a State of Michigan Landmark and listed on the National Register of Historic Places, the inn has survived the transformations that have unfolded over the past century.

In 1844, Alfred Ames envisioned a haven of recreation and tranquility, acquiring seventy-eight acres of land and establishing Ames Grove. By the 1890s, the Lakeside area had blossomed into a popular summer destination, attracting wealthy Chicago residents. Among them were Arthur Aylesworth and his brother, who were captivated by the area's natural beauty. In 1901, they persuaded their parents to purchase Ames Grove. John J. and Nancy E. Aylesworth also bought several other pieces of connecting land and built the Lakeside Inn and several cottages. Arthur eventually inherited the inn and operated it for many years.

Arthur Aylesworth, a man of multifaceted interests, infused the Lakeside Inn with his passion for sports, nature, and conservation. His zoo, a popular attraction, showcased an array of wildlife, from ringneck pheasants to Canada geese, and even featured an unusual breed of black raccoons. The inn's grounds were transformed into a haven for recreation, with tennis courts, a golf course, and a swimming pool adding to its allure.

As the Roaring Twenties unfolded, the Lakeside Inn became a hub of clandestine activities, its grand ballroom echoing with the strains of live music from Chicago orchestras. During the era of Prohibition, the inn became a haven for illicit gambling and the illegal exchange of alcohol. Rumors abound of Al Capone, the notorious gangster, frequenting the inn, adding a touch of intrigue to its history.

Arthur Aylesworth's first wife, Grace Garrett, was the aunt of silent film star Clara Kimball Young and a manager for actress Virginia Harned. Grace's theatrical talents eventually extended to her own stock company, the Aylesworth Stock Company, with which she toured as a dramatic actress for over three decades. She passed away in Los Angeles in 1959.

Arthur's second wife, Ida Prodie, passed away in 1953 at the inn after a prolonged illness. Her death is shrouded in mystery, with rumors persisting that Arthur was involved. It is said that Arthur "accidentally" shot her. Some stories even speculate that he murdered her. While Ida did pass away on the premises, she was not murdered. Murder makes for an interesting ghost story, but no one knows why Ida's spirit may still haunt the halls. However, in the 1990s, during renovations, workers found a bloodstained towel hidden in the walls embroidered with the name "Aylesworth." Something odd must have happened; why else would "evidence" be hidden in the wall?

Arthur sadly lost Lakeside to foreclosure by the Niles Bank. He passed away in 1962 at the University Hospital in Ann Arbor, where no one knew of his background. He almost became a medical cadaver until a doctor mentioned, during a phone conversation with Lakeside's township lawyer, that one of Lakeside's residents had passed away at the hospital. A few Lakeside residents drove to Ann Arbor, claimed his body, and brought him home so he could be buried in Lakeside Cemetery with his wife Ida.

For a while, Lakeside was known as the Lakeside Park Country Club and required membership. From 1968 to 1994, the Lakeside Center for the Arts occupied the premises. In 1995, it was restored to its 1920s appearance and opened as the Lakeside Inn.

The Lakeside Inn's rich history and tales of intrigue have given rise to numerous ghost stories. Arthur and Ida are the two spirits most often spotted

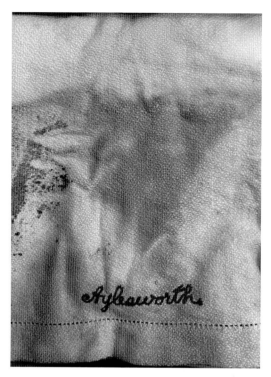

Left: The Aylesworth bloodstained towel. *Photo provided by Sam Darrigrand, Lakeside innkeeper.*

Below: Present-day view of Lakeside Inn. *Photo provided by Sam Darrigrand, Lakeside innkeeper.*

at the inn. They are not malevolent entities but rather spirits connected to the place they cherished. Ida's passing was a somber chapter in the inn's history, but her warm and welcoming spectral presence lingers within its walls. Arthur's spirit continues to wander the land of the place he loved most. Guests have reported hearing footsteps in empty corridors, witnessing doors opening and closing on their own, and experiencing strange occurrences in room 30, the designated "ghost room." One guest reported an encounter with Arthur's spectral form, accompanied by his beloved raccoon. Ida's gentle presence once urged a handyman to ensure Arthur's well-being.

The Lakeside Inn, with its blend of history, elegance, and a touch of the paranormal, offers an unforgettable experience for those seeking a glimpse into the past. Relax on the porch, soak in the serenity of the lakefront, and perhaps catch a glimpse of Arthur's or Ida's spirits.

Spooky Thrills Drive Haunted Tourism

G hostly chills and historical thrills are sending shivers down spines—and boosting tourism dollars. Haunted tourism, a branch of dark tourism drawn to macabre history, is experiencing a massive surge, with attractions reporting up to a fivefold increase in visitors compared to 2022, according to a 2023 report by Passage.

This tourism trend, coined "dark tourism" in 1996 by Professor John Lennon, extends beyond JFK's assassination site or Auschwitz. It encompasses memorials and locations steeped in tragedy, death, and suffering, drawing travelers who are intrigued by the darker side of history.

The roots of the haunted tourism industry can be traced to the Victorian era, a time when theaters held public séances and ghost stories were told on Christmas Eve. It was an era steeped in death, so many turned to spiritualism to make contact to the other side. Jessica O'Hara, author of *The Philosophy of Horror*, said something similar happened in the United States after 9/11. Theaters full of mediums were replaced by paranormal TV shows like *Ghost Hunters*, *Ghost Adventures*, and *The Dead Files*. These shows created interest in paranormal investigations, and a new wave of haunted tourism was born.

Savvy business owners are harnessing this fascination, not just for thrills, but for preservation. The ghost niche proves profitable, with haunted attractions in the United States alone pulling in over $300 million annually, according to estimates by America Haunts. Some ghostly giants capitalize on their haunted history to lure customers in with promises of thrills and chills, like the *Queen Mary* ($55 million revenue in 2022), the Stanley Hotel ($18 million), and the Crescent Hotel (a staggering $570 million).

Beyond financial gain, haunted tourism can breathe new life into forgotten venues. A 2020 *Cornell Hospitality Quarterly* study highlights how haunted attractions have saved abandoned hospitals, schools, and prisons from demolition, securing funds for needed renovations. Struggling small businesses like haunted inns, mansions, and historical house museums are also finding salvation by offering guests spooky experiences. Smart business owners are using paranormal tourism dollars to fund their historical preservation efforts.

The global dark tourism market is estimated to reach a chilling $36.5 billion by 2032, showcasing the increasing allure of macabre history.

Your fascination with all things spooky can help historical locations thrive and small businesses stay in business. So please, stay spooky and continue to enjoy your haunted travels.

BIBLIOGRAPHY

BOOKS

Arno Lyons, Sandy. *Michigan's Most Haunted*. Troy, MI: SkateRight Publishing, 2007.

Beauchamp, Nicole. *Haunted Bars & Pubs of Michigan*. Charleston, SC: The History Press, 2023.

Billock, Jennifer. *Ghosts of Michigan's Upper Peninsula*. Charleston, SC: Arcadia Publishing, 2018.

Blair, Brad, Tim Ellis, and Steve LaPlaunt. *Yoopernatural Haunts*. New Milford, CT: Visionary Living Publishing, 2019.

Clements, Todd. *Haunts of Mackinac: Ghost Stories, Legends, & Tragic Tales of Mackinac Island*. Grosse Point, MI: House of Hawthorne Publishing, 2006.

Higgs Stampfler, Dianna. *Michigan's Haunted Lighthouses*. Charleston, SC: The History Press, 2019.

Mason, Brian. *Haunted Marshall*. Pinckney, MI; Wynwidyn Press, 2017.

Milan, John, and Gail Offen. *Michigan Haunts: Public Places, Eerie Spaces*. Charleston, SC: Arcadia Publishing, 2019.

Moyet, Francois L., and Shirley A. Swift. *Henderson Castle: Kalamazoo's Legacy 1895–2013*. Kalamazoo, MI: Superior Professional Services, 2013.

Pattskyn, Helen. *Ghosthunting Michigan*. Covington, KY: Clerisy Press, 2012.

Tedsen, Kathleen, and Beverlee Ryden. *Haunted Travels of Michigan*. Holt, MI: Thunder Bay Press, 2008.

———. *Haunted Travels of Michigan.* Vol. 3, *Spirits Rising.* Holt, MI: Thunder Bay Press, 2013.

Weller, Theresa A. *The Founding Mothers of Mackinac Island.* East Lansing: University of Michigan Press, 2021.

WEBSITES

Adkins, Jeff, and Bonner, Todd. "These Are the Most Haunted Michigan Bars, Restaurants, According to Detroit Ghost Hunters." WDIV, October 5, 2022. www.clickondetroit.com/features/2022/10/05/these-are-the-most-haunted-michigan-bars-restaurants-according-to-detroit-ghost-hunters.

Associated Press. "The English Inn: History and Beauty in One Place." FOX 47 News Lansing-Jackson (WSYM), February 20, 2020. www.fox47news.com/news/michigan-made/the-english-inn-history-and-beauty-in-one-place.

Atlas Obscura. "The Hippie Tree." August 8, 2017. www.atlasobscura.com/places/the-hippie-tree-traverse-city-michigan.

The Blair Rick Project. "Sharing a Bed with a Ghost at Murphy Inn!" YouTube, August 18, 2023. youtu.be/q-wE8ZatQH0?si=QN6kolTLhCc93ppM.

Bloomberg.com. "Tapping Popular Ghost Tours for Historic Buildings Preservation." October 28, 2021. www.bloomberg.com/news/features/2021-10-28/when-ghost-hunters-become-historic-preservationists.

CBS News. "Powerhouse Co-Founder's Son Convicted in Killing." November 1, 2010. www.cbsnews.com/detroit/news/powerhouse-co-founders-son-convicted-in-killing.

The Gander, Michigan's Newsroom. "9 Things You Didn't Know about the Old Northern Michigan Asylum." January 11, 2023. gandernewsroom.com/2023/01/11/9-things-you-didnt-know-about-the-old-northern-michigan-asylum.

GhostQuest.net. "Haunted Locations: Big Bay, Michigan." www.ghostquest.net/haunted-places-big-bay-michigan.html.

GRAVE. "Thunder Bay Inn in Big Bay, MI." January 31, 2023. graveparanormal.com/thunder-bay-inn-in-big-bay-mi.

GRAVE Paranormal. "Thunder Bay Inn." YouTube, December 2, 2019. www.youtube.com/watch?v=qJ8d0DblK1s&t=9s.

Haunted Rooms America. "Haunted Traverse City State Hospital, MI." March 26, 2023. www.hauntedrooms.com/michigan/haunted-places/traverse-city-state-hospital.

Haunted US. "Discover Haunted Legends at the National House Inn Michigan's Oldest Hotel." November 22, 2023. hauntedus.com/michigan/national-house-inn.

Hayden, Martha. "Insane Asylum Part One History." The Restless Viking, October 20, 2021. www.restless-viking.com/2020/11/19/insane-asylum-part-one-history.

Heffner, Matt, and Andy Hawkins. "Historical & Haunted? The Traverse City State Hospital." Awesome Mitten, November 4, 2022. www.awesomemitten.com/traverse-city-state-hospital.

HistoricDetroit.org. "Fort Shelby Hotel: Historic Detroit." historicdetroit.org/buildings/fort-shelby-hotel.

HubPages. "The English Inn: A New Use for a Country Estate." July 5, 2019. hubpages.com/education/The-English-Inn-a-new-use-for-a-country-estate.

Journey with Murphy. "Traverse City State Hospital & the Hippie Tree." February 6, 2022. journeywithmurphy.com/2020/09/traverse-city-state-hospital-the-hippie-tree.

Lyons, Mickey. "Detroit Bars That Are Totally, Definitely Haunted." Thrillist, October 31, 2016. www.thrillist.com/drink/detroit/haunted-bars-in-detroit-michigan.

———. "Spirited Stories in Detroit Bars." *Hour Detroit Magazine*, October 4, 2022. www.hourdetroit.com/restaurants-bars/spirited-stories-in-detroit-bars/.

MichiganHauntedHouses.com. "Fort Shelby Doubletree Suites Hotel." www.michiganhauntedhouses.com/real-haunt/fort-shelby-doubletree-suites-hotel.html.

Munzenrieder, Kyle. "Peter Dabish Sentenced to Life for Torture and Murder of Recent UM Grad Diana DeMayo." *Miami New Times*, November 19, 2010. www.miaminewtimes.com/news/peter-dabish-sentenced-to-life-for-torture-and-murder-of-recent-um-grad-diana-demayo-6548457.

Mysterious Michigan. "Haunted Traverse City State Hospital." August 8, 2022. mysteriousmichigan.com/haunted-traverse-city-state-hospital.

National Storage. "Haunted Detroit." December 16, 2020. storenational. com/blog/haunted-detroit.

Newspapers.com. *Detroit Free Press*, April 8, 2010, 6. www.newspapers.com/ image/363372569.

———. *Detroit Free Press*, April 9, 2010, 11. www.newspapers.com/ image/363374477.

———. *Detroit Free Press*, November 2, 2010, 3. www.newspapers.com/ image/363812745.

Newsroom, WPBN/WGTU. "Haunted Northern Michigan: The Cottonwood Inn." upnorthlive.com/news/local/haunted-northern-michigan-the-cottonwood-inn.

910News.com. "Inside the Haunted Terrace Inn in Petoskey." www.9and10news.com/2018/10/26/inside-the-haunted-terrace-inn-in-petoskey.

Northern Express. "Thunder Bay Inn." www.northernexpress.com/news/ feature/thunder-bay-inn.

Obscure American History. "The Man Who Put Yellowstone National Park on the Map: Philetus W. Norris." obscureamericanhistory.blogspot. com/2011/09/man-who-put-yellowstone-national-park.html.

OnlyInYourState. "Stay Overnight in a 104-Year-Old Hotel That's Said to Be Haunted at Fort Shelby Hotel in Detroit." November 16, 2020. www.onlyinyourstate.com/michigan/detroit/fort-shelby-haunted-hotel-detroit-mi.

Petoskey News-Review. "Scary Stories of Petoskey's Perry Hotel." October 24, 2019. www.petoskeynews.com/story/entertainment/2019/10/24/ scary-stories-of-petoskeys-perry-hotel/44221605.

Phillips, Dave. "Son of Powerhouse Gym Co-Founder Held without Bond in Murder Case." *Oakland Press*, June 17, 2021. www.theoaklandpress. com/2010/04/08/son-of-powerhouse-gym-co-founder-held-without-bond-in-murder-case.

Prohibition Detroit. "Tinker, Tailor, Soldier, Spy: Two Way Inn." prohibitiondetroit.com/web/tinker-tailor-soldier-spy-two-way-inn.

Pure Michigan, Official Travel & Tourism Website for Michigan. "12 Incredibly Haunted Places in the Upper Peninsula." August 29, 2023. www.michigan.org/article/trip-idea/incredibly-haunted-places-upper-peninsula.

Robinson, John. "Haunted Michigan: Traverse City's 'Portal to Hell.'" 99.1 WFMK, October 30, 2019. 99wfmk.com/portal-to-hell-hippie-tree.

———. "The Haunting of the Cottonwood Inn: Empire, Michigan (and the Sons Who Never Left)." The Game 730 AM WVFN, October 25, 2023. thegame730am.com/ixp/691/p/cottonwood-inn-haunted-empire.

———. "Two-Way Inn: The Oldest and Most Haunted Bar in Detroit, Michigan." 99.1 WFMK, October 31, 2023. 99wfmk.com/two-way-inn-the-oldest-and-most-haunted-bar-in-detroit-michigan.

Scaramuzzino, Annie. "Beer, Wine and 'Spirits': The Oldest Bar in Detroit May Also Be the Most Haunted." October 14, 2022. www.audacy.com/wwjnewsradio/news/local/beer-wine-and-spirits-the-oldest-bar-in-detroit-may-also-be-the-most-haunted.

Svoboda, Sandra. "A Spirit of Detroit." *Detroit Metro Times*, September 1, 2023. www.metrotimes.com/news/a-spirit-of-detroit-2192081.

Sylvain, Rick. "Murphy Inn in St. Clair Still Bustles." *Detroit Free Press*, May 18, 1986. www.newspapers.com/article/detroit-free-press/139031200.

Times Herald. "The Murphy Inn." October 23, 1995.

———. "Video: Is Murphy Inn Haunted?" www.thetimesherald.com/videos/news/2020/10/30/video-murphy-inn-haunted/6087700002.

whatsajosh. "Ghosts Shake Floors and Rattle Dishes in the Haunted Cottonwood Farmhouse [Full Movie]." YouTube, November 21, 2022. www.youtube.com/watch?v=_FLWMNTcHLA.

Women on the Road. "Ghost Tourism: The Thrill of Fear (without the Danger)." October 11, 2023. www.women-on-the-road.com/ghost-tourism.html.

ABOUT THE AUTHOR

Roxanne Rhoads is an author, book publicist, mixed media crafter, and lover of all things spooky. Her books include *Haunted Flint* and *Ghosts and Legends of Genesee and Lapeer Counties*.

She owns Bewitching Book Tours, a virtual book tour and social media marketing company, and she operates a Halloween blog, *A Bewitching Guide to Halloween*. She sells vintage treasures, handcrafted jewelry, art, and home decor through her Etsy store, the Bewitching Cauldron, and in her antique booth, Bewitching Vintage Treasures.

When not reading or writing, Roxanne loves to craft, plan Halloween adventures, and search for unique vintage finds.

FREE eBOOK OFFER

Scan the QR code below, enter your e-mail address and get our original Haunted America compilation eBook delivered straight to your inbox for free.

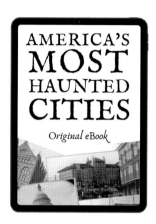

ABOUT THE BOOK

Every city, town, parish, community and school has their own paranormal history. Whether they are spirits caught in the Bardo, ancestors checking on their descendants, restless souls sending a message or simply spectral troublemakers, ghosts have been part of the human tradition from the beginning of time.

In this book, we feature a collection of stories from five of America's most haunted cities: Baltimore, Chicago, Galveston, New Orleans and Washington, D.C.

SCAN TO GET
AMERICA'S MOST HAUNTED CITIES

Having trouble scanning? Go to:
biz.arcadiapublishing.com/americas-most-haunted-cities